Introduction

Dr. Otto A. Piper, grand New Testament scholar at Princeton Theological Seminary for many years, impressed most deeply upon me that Christianity is not following rules and laws, but it is a relationship. I had been taught that we are saved by faith in Jesus Christ since childhood, but somehow the dots had never been so clearly connected. Dr. Piper helped me understand that putting faith in Jesus Christ is entering a relationship with Jesus Christ.

Developing this relationship has been a life long pursuit of mine, and I have come to realize that it is a daily experience. Relating to God from Monday to Friday is essential for your relationship with God to be intimate and complete. Weekend corporate worship is wonderful and necessary in this relationship, but it is inadequate apart from the personal experience one needs alone with Jesus Christ.

In order to have spiritual passion, it is important to commune with God daily and alone. Along with our arrow prayers and conversation with God throughout the day, it is important to have a personal, quiet time with God every day. Most Christians are able to do this best in their homes, while some find it most convenient at their offices.

One man said he had his solitude with God in his car during lunch break at work.

As we relate with Jesus Christ, we naturally talk with him. But, as a relationship is between two persons, it also involves listening. As we share our thanksgivings, confessions and concerns with Christ through prayer, God speaks to us directly through the Holy Spirit as well as through God's written word, the Bible. Reading God's word enlightens us, guides us, comforts us and strengthens us.

This little book, **100 Days of Hope**, centers your mind on a small portion of scripture, and then it provides thoughts about it. The devotional for each day ends with a prayer and a thought for the day.

The focus of this book is hope. God has great hope for your life, and God needs for you to have hope as well. Life is filled with great joy and accomplishment, when the heart is full of hope. As God is the God of all of life, God wants you to have hope in all circumstances. Hope covering many of life's experiences is offered in these pages.

It is my prayer that this book will provide you with wonderful new hope that will bring you blessings beyond your understanding. I also pray that you will develop deep passion for the glorious goodness available from God through faith in Jesus Christ.

100 Days of Hope

Igniting Your Passion For God

ROYAL SPEIDEL

ChurchSmart
RESOURCES

St. Charles, IL 60174
1-800-253-4276

Published by ChurchSmart Resources

We are an evangelical Christian publisher committed to producing excellent products at affordable prices to help church leaders accomplish effective ministry in the areas of Church planting, Church growth, Church renewal and Leadership development.

For a free catalog of our resources call 1-800-253-4276.
Visit us at: *www.churchsmart.com*

Cover design by: Julie Becker

© Copyright 2007 by Royal Speidel

ISBN#: 1-889638-65-X

100 Days of Hope

Dedication

To two wonderful prayer partners
Rita for 39 years
Evelyn for 2 years

Day 1

Hope in Having Choices

"The people said to Joshua, 'The Lord our God we will serve,
and him we will obey." Joshua 24:24

As we move through the days, weeks and months of each year, our spiritual strength will be determined by the choices we make. Just as choosing what kind of food we eat, and whether we exercise or not, determines our health condition, so our life choices create our spiritual condition. There is hope that we will make good choices.

When Joshua led the Israelite people into the Promised Land, he said to them, "Now therefore revere the Lord, and serve him in sincerity and in faithfulness; put away the gods that your ancestors served...Choose this day whom you will serve..." (Joshua 24:14) Those same words come to us from Joshua daily as we step across new thresholds of time. The people of Israel were surrounded by temptations to follow the many gods of their day, and we, too, have many gods seeking our attention. Choose every day this year whom you will serve.

The good news behind Joshua's words, "choose this day," is that God empowers us to decide the directions of our lives. The gift of choice is one of the most basic graces God gave us. Instead of looking at choice as a labor of having to make decisions, it is an exciting privilege to choose the paths we wish to take in life.

It is thrilling to rise in the morning knowing we have a whole day to make choices: how we will spend our time, what kind of activities we will engage, the kinds of relationships we will enter, and how we will invest our resources. The Christian knows the basis for all choices is wanting the will of God. Doing the will of God gives us the best life possible.

We do not make decisions, and then ask God to bless them. Rather, *before we decide*, we ask God to help us make decisions that God will bless.

Joshua said, "Choose this day whom you will serve."

$\approx\!\approx\!\approx$

Dear God, thank you for freedom to make decisions. It is a great gift of love that you trust us so much to make choices. Help me today as I use the privilege of choosing the direction my life takes, and Holy Spirit, guide me to choose wisely. In Jesus' name. Amen

Can I rejoice in my privilege of making decisions, and grow to make wise choices?

Hope in My Significance

"For all who are led by the Spirit of God are children of God."
Romans 8:14

Two thousand years ago, a young Jewish man named Saul was on the road to the city of Damascus. Saul reported of that day, "While I was on my way and approaching Damascus, about noon a great light from heaven suddenly shone about me. I fell to the ground and heard a voice saying to me, "Saul, Saul, why are you persecuting me?" I answered, "Who are you, Lord?" Then he said to me, "I am Jesus of Nazareth whom you are persecuting." (Acts 22:6-8) As if struck by a bolt of lightening, Saul was knocked to the ground. Jesus certainly got Saul's attention! Temporarily blinded, he was led to the house of a Christian named Ananias who restored his sight.

That experience radically changed the direction of Saul's life. Previously, he had persecuted Christians for worshipping Jesus Christ, now he began preaching new life in Jesus. Even though Saul, now known as Paul, would suffer many hardships for following Jesus, this new direction of life gave him enormous meaning and peace.

God wants your life to have great meaning. You were made for a purpose. As with Paul, our first circle of life is found in God through Jesus Christ. Once in that divine loop, God guides us to a life of exciting fulfillment. That guidance rarely strikes us like lightning, but with a quiet, surging movement of the Holy Spirit.

The most important aspect of living is to find that role for which God created you. What is it that God wants you to do with your life? Where should you apply your talents? How can you best spend your time? God will fill you with the deepest satisfaction and greatest joys in life as you learn to answer those questions.

✒ ✒ ✒

Creator God, thank you for making my life to have purpose. There is a niche in creation you need me to fill. Guide me to it, so my life can have fulfillment. I praise you that my life means something to you and to the world. In Jesus' name. Amen

Am I looking for the role God has for me? After finding it, will I accept it?

Hope of Blooming
Where You are Planted

"Jesus had just then cured many people of diseases, plagues, and evil spirits, and had given sight to many who were blind." Luke 7:21

Jesus came into the world to redeem humankind. He poured himself into his work without reserve, often until he was very tired. Completely human although divine, serving took its toll on Jesus, just like it does on us. Yet he invested his life to fulfill God's purpose.

People sometimes wonder if they are doing God's will in what seems a mundane daily existence. They think God's will is only performing some grandiose ministry. But God delights in the smaller things of daily life as well. God has a plan for you, and it is wonderfully exciting and fulfilling to bloom where God plants us. Start with family. If you are a wife or husband and have children, God calls you to invest yourself fully in that relationship.

Supporting a spouse with loving care and attention is lifting up the life partner God has put into our care. Ministering to your children is allowing God to help build tender lives, who as adults will be much stronger and wiser because of your caring. It is God's plan for everyone to take care of his or her family. Couples without children find much fulfillment in giving themselves to nieces and nephews or in mentoring other youth.

What about your profession? What is God's will for you concerning work? What am I to do with my life? As long as it is godly work, you enjoy it, and it gives you the money you need, then it certainly fits in with God's basic plan. Someone may ask, "Is working for a hamburger restaurant, a telephone company, or making plastics in a factory godly work?" These jobs contribute to the good of society, so they are godly tasks. You ought to be able to look at your work as a ministry. Think of doing your work not just for your boss but for Jesus. It will make a world of difference in your attitude as you go to work every day.

Dear God, help me today to feel great about where I am. Enable me to be happy loving my family, and allow my work to fill me with deep satisfaction. In Jesus' name. Amen

How can I blossom in the place I am planted?

Hope for Total Self-giving

"For this I toil and struggle with all the energy that he powerfully inspires within me." Colossians 1:29

The apostle Paul wrote those words to the Christians in the church at Colossae about his work at making "the word of God fully known" to them. He gave himself without reservation to helping others find new life in Jesus Christ, and became a great model for other disciples of Jesus Christ throughout the history of the church. There is great hope in laying down our lives in service for Jesus Christ. Paul no doubt did what he heard that Jesus had done.

Jesus himself set a great example with his works. God spoke to Jesus through an overshadowing cloud saying, "This is my Son, the Beloved, with him I am well pleased; listen to him." (Matthew 17:5) Jesus was pleasing to God, not only for who he was, but also for what he did. His work was an extension of his being. He was totally involved in his ministry of self-giving for God.

Paul wrote to his young colleague, Timothy, to tell his congregation, "They are to do good, to be rich in good works," (I Timothy 6:18a) He wrote to Titus, "Show yourself in all respects a model of good works," (2:7a) A chapter later he wrote to Titus, "I desire that you insist on these things, so that those who have come to believe in God may be careful to devote themselves to good works; these are excellent and profitable to everyone." (3:8) God indeed created us to give ourselves in devotion to serve others.

We find great fulfillment in self-investment, and the joyous sense of accomplishment it brings us. It is a great privilege to lay down our lives for Jesus Christ, because God rewards us both in this world and the next. To focus our thoughts and expend energies ministering for Jesus Christ pacifies the heart with a deep satisfaction. Nothing in life can bring the profound sense of joy found in giving ourselves for God's work.

This expenditure of self brings hope, and those wishing to have this single-minded life of self-giving can have this hope. It is available to all. It is the self-giving that does good works for God and God's world.

Gracious God, thank you for the privilege of giving myself, and for the wonderful fulfillment that comes from it. Bless me with greater understanding of how I can give myself more fully. In Jesus' name. Amen

How can I lay down my life more completely for Jesus Christ?

Hope for Godliness

"Therefore be imitators of God as beloved children, and live in love as Christ loved us and gave himself up for us, a fragrant offering and sacrifice to God." Ephesians 5:1-2

Since we were created in God's image, there is an innate desire deep in every human heart to be like the one who made us. But, how do we get that way? Is there hope for godliness?

The Christian gospel is full of hope to become like God in our behavior. Paul wrote to Jesus' followers in the city of Ephesus, "Therefore be imitators of God as beloved children, and live in love as Christ loved us and gave himself up for us, a fragrant offering and sacrifice to God." (Ephesians 5:1)

Paul believed in the hope for godliness. He challenged the Ephesian Christians to follow the highest standard in the whole world — to be imitators of God. The Greek word for imitation, *mimesis*, was a very well known term to the Greeks. It was used in training an orator. To be a great orator, you must learn to imitate the great orators. Paul wrote that if you plan to be great at living life, you must learn to imitate the Lord of life.

It is common these days to hire coaches to help us. Young athletes in training hire experts who can help them achieve their best. In addition to helping athletes excel, the coaches become cheerleaders who lift the spirits of their young prodigies. When the young athletes fall, the coaches pick them up. Knowing that utter commitment is necessary for excellence, the coaches prod and goad the young people into reaching to the depth of their spirits.

Christians have a life coach in Jesus Christ, who enhances our personal effectiveness. He is our personal trainer in the University of Life, who will help us achieve the highest awards. A changed man said, "Since I accepted Jesus Christ as my savior 38 years ago, the Holy Spirit has been my coach." Paul told the Christians in Philippi, "Let the same mind be in you that was in Christ Jesus...." (Philippians 2:5) Allowing Christ to be our coach gives us hope at being filled with godliness.

Almighty God, we thank you for the high standard of love you hold for us, and are grateful for the privilege of imitating your love. Help me to imitate you, so my life can be a "fragrant offering" to you and to the world. In Jesus' name. Amen

What will I be like if godliness saturates my life?

Hope for Living Wisely

"If any of you is lacking in wisdom, ask God, who gives to all generously and ungrudgingly, and it will be given you." James 1:5

Living life fully and well requires living wisely. The book of Proverbs offers this redundancy: "The beginning of wisdom is this: Get wisdom." (4:7a) Although knowledge can be helpful in living wisely, wisdom is different and is more important than simply acquiring information. Wisdom is not the product of academic achievement or class standings; wisdom has to do with relationships and caring for life. It has to do with relating to God, self and others.

Wisdom includes humility, discipline and avoiding evil which has been prevalent in every age. Evil existed in the time of the Ephesian Christians as it does today. So the words Paul wrote to them are still very applicable to us: "Be careful then how you live, not as unwise people but as wise." (5:15) Great temptation surrounds people in every culture. Peter wrote in his first letter, "Discipline yourselves, keep alert, like a roaring lion your adversary the devil prowls around, looking for someone to devour." (5:8) Without using the word, he was admonishing us to live wisely.

God is not only omniscient, but also all wise. In God we find understanding and insight on how to live, and God is very open to sharing wisdom with us. As God's children, God wants deeply to help us live life effectively and joyously. So James wrote, "If any of you is lacking in wisdom, ask God, who gives to all generously and ungrudgingly, and it will be given you." (1:5)

Paul wrote, "And we speak of those things in words not taught by human wisdom but taught by the Spirit..." (I Corinthians 2:13a) Jesus said the Holy Spirit would be a guide and counselor to us as we open our lives to divine guidance. There is great hope for wisdom in your life. If you ask God for wisdom through prayer, God will grant it.

All wise God, thank you for your desire that I be a wise person. I am grateful you want to share understanding with me to help me live life most effectively. Give me wisdom for the living of this day. In Jesus' name. Amen

Where do I need more wisdom for living?

Hope in the Midst of Grief

*"For the wages of sin is death, but the free gift of God is eternal life
in Christ Jesus our Lord." Romans 6:23*

We all face death during life because death is part of life. Eternal life for Paul was a gift that began, not at death, but at the point of trusting Christ. The Christian can relax in the arms of God with the assurance of having eternal life now. That frees us from fear of death and liberates us to live life most fully.

I write these words three weeks after losing my wife of 39 years. Death can be seen as a thief who steals life from us. Fathers, mothers, husbands, wives, sisters, brothers, and perhaps worst of all, sons and daughters. Death stole parents from thousands of children on September 11, 2001. Annually it breaks up life-long marriages. Its stranglehold on parents who lose children is so strong it often destroys their relationship.

Death reddens the eyes and stains the cheeks with tears. Out of the depth of the soul that has not wept for decades come sobs of sadness and grief. We are seemingly rendered helpless in the face of death, but not without hope.

God's promise of eternal life in Jesus Christ is our first and great hope. It's glorious to know our loved ones have graduated into a more beautiful and wonderful life. It comforts our pain. This helps us realize we do not cry for our loved ones, but for ourselves. They have reached the land where crying and tears are no more, and where the sun does not set, because there is no darkness.

Jesus said he would send a comforter, the Holy Spirit, who in his sweetness brings gradual relief. It needs to be slow to be natural. Instant relief from grief would be artificial. Lingering grief is a normal part of evolving from the loss of a deep relationship.

Dear God, thank you for the one I have lost, and thank you for receiving my loved one into your eternal arms. Utterly grateful for the blessing of our relationship, I now receive your gracious healing in this loss. In Jesus' name. Amen

God's loving arms enfold us during loss through death in this life, and will embrace us with wonder in the next.

Day 8

Hope in Serving Others

"Now there are varieties of gifts, but the same Spirit; and there are varieties of services, but the same Lord; and there are varieties of activities, but it is the same God who activates all of them in every one."
I Corinthians 12:4-6

There is great hope in giving ourselves in service to others, as that gift brings us joy and satisfaction. People caught up only in themselves are often unhappy and unfulfilled. The waters of self are very shallow and being confined to them commonly troubles the soul. The Holy Spirit's way out of this stagnancy is to begin serving others.

People of all ages find new life in self-giving. Young people are energized as they give themselves in serving others. At the other end of the age spectrum many senior citizens feel they literally live longer volunteering their time and energy in hospitals and schools. Even the middle aged in the midst of raising their own children realize God adds to their lives when they serve others.

God has given you spiritual gifts that are part of your destiny. The Bible mentions 25 of them. Paul wrote to the Christians in the city of Corinth, "Now there are varieties of gifts, but this same Spirit; and there are varieties of services, but the same Lord."

Some have the gift of teaching, which can help people understand Christian truth. Some have a gift of compassion able to give deep and warm caring. Those who have the gift of service know how to give themselves helping others. Those with the gift of leadership know how to organize life and help God's work administratively. God has blessed some with a special gift to make money, and God uses their giving to support many ministries.

All who walk by the name of Jesus are enriched by giving themselves in ministry for Jesus. This is your destiny. It is God's plan for you. Paul wrote "the same God who (gave your gifts) activates all of them in everyone." (I Corinthians 12:6b) Two questions: Do you know the spiritual gifts God has given you? Are you using them to serve God's kingdom?

Dear God, thank you for giving me gifts to be used in serving others. This self-giving enlivens hope within me, and gives new life to me and to others. Thank you. In Jesus' name. Amen

There is new hope as I lay down my life for Jesus.

Hope in Guidance from God

"Joseph, son of David, do not be afraid to take Mary as your wife,
for the child conceived in her is from the Holy Spirit." Matthew 1:20c

No person is totally independent, making decisions without any influence. Everyone is swayed in living his or her life. The only question is, "Who is influencing us?" "How are we being guided?" Hope for the best life comes from being directed by God.

Joseph was engaged to a young woman named Mary who probably was a teenager. Before they lived together or had a sexual relationship, Joseph learned she was pregnant. Matthew writes, "she was found to be with child from the Holy Spirit," but Joseph thought otherwise. He thought she had been unfaithful. How do men react when they find out their girlfriend is pregnant from another man? He considered rejecting her.

However, Joseph took his orders from God. Matthew writes, "Joseph, being a righteous man and unwilling to expose her to public disgrace, planned to dismiss her quietly." (Matthew 1:19) Joseph walked with God and knew God wants us to respect each other with dignity and grace. His behavior, plan book, and direction came from God. He would not publicly embarrass Mary.

But God even gave him more directions: Matthew writes, "But just when he had resolved to do this, an angel of the Lord appeared to him in a dream and said, 'Joseph, son of David, do not be afraid to take Mary as your wife, for the child conceived in her is from the Holy Spirit.'" (Matthew 1:20)

God may not speak to us in dreams or through a burning bush as God spoke to Moses; however, God is still guiding us in our daily affairs. Most often the Holy Spirit leads us by our private thoughts if we are centered on doing God's will. All of us have to deal with making personal and private decisions, but if we make them solely based on ourselves we will get into trouble. We are guided to make the best decisions, when we open our minds to God.

God also uses people to affect us. In the book of Proverbs, God tells us there is wisdom in many counselors. Consulting with others ensures that we are on the right track. Sometimes God uses other people to help us understand the handwriting of God's instructions for us more clearly. The most fundamental direction from God comes through the Bible. God has used this treasured book to form societies and civilizations, and it is a great guide for us.

✢ ✢ ✢

All wise God, thank you for being available to guide me. Life is so much more secure knowing I am walking in your path. Help me to seek your guidance today, so my life can be best lived. In Jesus' name. Amen

I want to be guided in all of my thoughts and actions by God.

Hope in Being Honest with God

"Create in me a clean heart, O God, and put a new and right spirit within me." Psalm 51:10

Being honest with our self and with God is one of the most difficult things in life. Our emotional biases blur our weaknesses, so we overlook areas of failure and need. Coming to know our real selves before God is a wonderful gift, giving us hope. We receive hope for the future while we live in reality.

The prophet Nathan challenged King David to be honest before God. The story of King David having a romantic fling with Bathsheba is well known. Bathsheba was the only wife of a very principled man named Uriah. In contrast, David had many, many wives, but he coveted Bathsheba. David acted like a demon instead of a king because he not only stole Bathsheba, Uriah's only wife, but also had Uriah murdered to cover up his sin.

Nathan was a man of God sent to confront David. He told the king there were two men in a city: one was rich and the other poor. The rich man had huge flocks of sheep and herds of other animals. The poor man owned only a little lamb. That little ewe lamb was like a child to that family. The poor man actually had the lamb drink milk from his cup, and the Bible says, "it would lie in his bosom, and it was like a daughter to him." A friend came a long distance to visit the rich man, who wanted to treat his distant friend to a special meal. Despite owning hundreds of sheep, he didn't want to kill any of them, so he stole the only sheep the poor man had. Using that little lamb he made a special meal for his traveling guest.

When King David heard this story he was outraged. In his anger he said to the prophet, Nathan, "As the Lord lives, the man who has done this deserves to die; he shall restore the lamb fourfold, because he did this thing, and because he had no pity. Nathan said to David, "You are the man!" (2 Samuel 12:5c,6) David then confessed his sin and was cleansed.

Being honest before God is a great blessing and gives us hope living with integrity. It unburdens us of stifling guilt, which blankets a happy personality. Guilt takes the smile from a joyous heart, triggers anger and distorts thinking. It can hurt relationships. Carrying around guilt on your shoulders can become a heavy burden, and living with a person whose spirit is twisted by guilt can be an unhappy experience. Being honest before God cleanses us and sets us free giving us new life.

෴෴෴

Dear God, I want to be honest with you and with myself. Hold a mirror before me, so I can see who I really am. Where I have failed, please forgive me and set me free. In Jesus' name. Amen

I want to be humbly honest before God.

Hope to Become a Complete Person

"May the God of peace himself sanctify you entirely; and may your spirit and souls and body be kept sound and blameless at the coming of our Lord Jesus Christ." 1 Thessalonians 5:23

As sincere Christians, we show our thanksgiving to God by trying to do the will of God in all things and by trying to become the very best people we can become. We have hope to become the finest, most intentional Christians possible. In theology this is called sanctification. To be sanctified is to be set apart for a holy purpose. It is to be set apart for God. Sanctified people are fully consecrated to God, completely dedicated to doing God's will.

Paul wrote to the Christians in Ephesus, "Christ loved the church and gave himself up for her, in order to make her holy..." The word "holy" means sanctified, set apart. Christ sanctified the church by dying for her. He set the church apart to be fully dedicated to God. The church of Jesus Christ is to be consecrated to God like no other organization on earth.

When we come to Jesus Christ, God consecrates us and sets us apart for godly living. We are to be different than the world. Our values are now the values of heaven instead of the values of earth. We walk to the beat of a heavenly drummer instead of the humdrum noise of the world.

To be sanctified means to be a complete person. Even though I work out at the health club on fourteen weight machines and the bicycle, my children have encouraged me to get into stretching. I asked the fitness counselor at the health club about it. She said by working with weight machines, riding the bicycle and then stretching you will have a complete body. Muscles will be strong, the cardio-vascular system is healthy and stretching gives the body flexibility. God wants you and me to be complete people — not only physically but also spiritually.

This spiritual fullness comes as we live closely with God. The closer we grow to God, the more distasteful sin becomes. The light of Christ exposes the dark corners of disobedience within our souls. God's power through the Holy Spirit enables us to overcome negative patterns and develop more heavenly grace.

✥ ✥ ✥

Gracious and righteous God, thank you for giving us the gift of sanctification, for setting us apart to be lovingly different than the world. I praise you for the power of the Holy Spirit to help me be a more complete, spiritual person. In Jesus' name. Amen

I want to grow as close to God as I can, so God can help me become all that I can.

Hope for New Beginnings

---

*"You were taught to put away your former way of life, your old self...
and to be renewed in the spirit of your minds, and to clothe yourselves
with the new self, created according to the likeness of God in true
righteousness and holiness." Ephesians 4:22*

New beginnings feel good because of their freshness. All of us yearn to begin again, without the blemishes of the past. Through our bad choices, the walls of life have developed ugly cracks, and the faded paint reminds us of empty spirits created by pain and rejection. If only we could recapture that new look associated with hope for a great today and a blessed tomorrow!

People often go to new places in order to start life over again. They expect a new location will create a new beginning. The old place is filled with memories of bad relationships. Painful memories are etched in the walls of the house. The hateful words spoken in that home have become part of the paint. Associations linger.

A wife remembers the kitchen where her husband yelled very hurtful words at her. Children recall lying in their beds, fearful as they heard their parents fighting in the darkened night. A father remembers a rocking chair where he used to sit, waiting anxiously for his children to come home safely in the early morning hours.

Open spaces all across America are filling up with new houses. Buildings replacing cornstalks everywhere are seen by new residents as symbols of new hope as places where new fruit will be born. Folks building these new homes are filled with hope for a new life, thinking a new home is a new beginning.

Unfortunately, hundreds of these families are not going to be fulfilled in their new homes, because they are bringing their old selves with them. They will find out new walls aren't the same as new hearts. Unhappily, the old family arguments in the last house will be transplanted to the new one. Changing addresses will not transform relationships.

Paul told the Philippians that only new hearts and new minds bring happy beginnings that renew relationships with warmth and joy. God wants to revitalize us with love and power filling our hearts, and leading us to be more victorious in our daily lives.

⚜⚜⚜

Dear God, thank you for being a God of new beginnings. I humble myself before you asking for things to be made new in my life, fresh and beautiful like the sunrise. In Jesus' name. Amen

I am excited to know God can make my life new today.

Day 13

Hope for a Model for Life

"Be perfect, therefore, as your heavenly Father is perfect." Matthew 5:48

When Jesus spoke these words, he had perfection of love in mind. He was not encouraging his followers to be perfect with matching the color of their clothing, having their haircut properly, keeping their houses clean or their yards neat. Jesus preceded this call to be perfect as our heavenly Father is perfect with an admonition to love our neighbors. He concluded as God is a perfectly loving God, we also ought to love perfectly. This makes God our model for loving, which is the essence of the Christian life. After giving our hearts to Jesus Christ and loving God with our whole beings, we are to spend our whole lives loving others. This means that God is to set the standard for our caring for others.

From a human standpoint, Christians are like all others in that we let people set our standards. Naturally, people around us shape our lives, and indeed, we are composite pictures painted by the people in our lives. It is important to be surrounded by loving persons after whom we can model our lives. People influence us at every age. Children are sponges, who absorb their surroundings. The early smile of a baby is simply a mimic of his or her parents. When words are formed in a child's mouth, they will be words heard from the Mom and Dad. Teenage behavior usually reflects what the teenager has seen in the home. Their associates influence even older adults. As strawberry Kool-Aid colors water red, so people around us change our lives. In addition to seeing love demonstrated by God, we need also to have loving influence from those around us. The godly example of love in family, friends and co-workers will enhance our ability to model our lives after the highest standard of love found in God.

But no matter how wonderful the people around us, Christians look to God as their standard bearer, when it comes to love. It is God's nature to love, so John even wrote, "God is love..." (I John 4:16c)

God's love includes action. When God saw his children enslaved to Egypt, he called Moses to lead them out of Egypt into freedom. When God saw Saul trying to kill David, he spared him. When God saw the people of Nineveh to be condemned for living in sin, he called Jonah to preach to them and help them escape judgment. When God saw the giant Goliath threatening the Israeli army, he sent the young shepherd David to destroy him.

✣ ✣ ✣

Thank you, Lord Jesus, for teaching us that God is our perfect model of love. I want your power, to model my life of loving after him. As God loved not only in word but also deed, help me to be caring in all I think, say and do. In your name. Amen

Modeling my life after God I will become more loving and kind.

Hope to Get Rid of Bad Stuff

"But fornication and impurity of any kind, or greed, must not even be mentioned among you, as is proper among saints." Ephesians 5:3

Temptation surrounds us from the childhood years of consciousness until the day we die. However, we have power to eliminate elements of it from our lives. When unwanted thoughts frustrate us, or when impulses for negative behavior tempt us, and we do not know how to rid ourselves of them, there is hope in God. God gives us the grace to be freed from evil.

Paul writes that we should not even discuss the possibility of engaging in impurity and greed. We should not waste our time discussing negative "stuff" put on our nation's airwaves through radio and television or brought into homes through the Internet. Sleaze is not worth talking about. It is wrong and sinful and nothing positive can come from talking about it.

Evil begins with the mind — the kinds of thoughts we think. If you want to become perfect in love, you need to fill your mind with loving thoughts. When you are preoccupied with goodness and kindness, there is no room for evil and hurtful thoughts. The closet of the mind can be cluttered with negative junk, or it can be ordered with wonderful, positive images.

The Holy Spirit fills us with hope to rid ourselves of sinful thoughts, words and behavior. You can free yourself from barnacles of negativity that would latch on to the boat of your life and slow you down. The best way to eliminate evil is to fill ourselves with God. When the mind is preoccupied with godly thoughts, the spirit is diverted away from evil.

Fighting temptation requires discipline. Living closely in fellowship with Jesus Christ provides self-control to keep evil from our lives. Focusing on Jesus Christ provides the focus to stay away from that which would hurt us or bring pain to others through us.

♫ ♫ ♫

Dear God, let me not flirt with impurity and greed, but give me courage and power to put it out of my life. Help me to separate myself from it, so I can know the wonder of your cleanliness and wholeness. In Jesus' name. Amen

Today I will keep my mind free from impure thoughts by filling it with godly love.

Hope for a Smooth Marriage

"Be subject to one another out of reverence for Christ." Ephesians 5:21

These words preface a great statement on marriage Paul wrote to the Christians in the city of Ephesus. Christians raised the level of marriage to a beautiful bond between a man and a woman. A Christian marriage is about mutual love and respect — caring for each other.

If love and respect exist, there will be regard for each other's thoughts and views. God seems to put together a lot of completely different people in marriage. During the early years of marriage, the differences are fun and interesting. As the years pass they often become frustrating and aggravating, but differences make for a strong and healthy marriage. Because we have opinions and preferences that vary, every successful marriage involves a lot of compromise, bending and willingness to submit to the other. We have to give in and let the other have his or her way just as we want ours. But it requires the grace of God to recognize the value of a different way of doing things, and being willing to bend to try that. Or, couples need to find agreeable compromise solutions.

Subjecting ourselves to each other is hard. The natural way of life is to stand up for our own desires and demand our own preferences. Bending to the will of the other is not easy.

Where do we receive such grace to want the will of the other? On our knees. Only God can melt a heart of steel and make pliable a hard, stubborn will. Humbling ourselves before Jesus Christ, and asking for grace and mercy softly transforms the desires of the heart. Many times in my marriage I knelt to pray after a marital dispute, and God opened my eyes to my role in the problem. Plus, God did it so gently.

God made marriages, and God wants them happy and peaceful. The Holy Spirit can lovingly make a bitter relationship sweet if, out of love for God, we are willing to yield to one another.

Dear God, thank you for hope for my marriage. I know you created it, and you want it full of joy and peace. Help me to humble myself before my spouse. In Jesus' name. Amen

I want a great marriage and know God will help me work at it.

Hope for Inner Peace

"Jesus said to them again, 'Peace be with you.
As the Father has sent me, so I send you.'" John 20:21

On the first Easter Sunday evening the disciples were in a house with locked doors fearing for their lives. Jesus appeared among them, and said, "Peace be with you." Numbed by his death, the disciples were now ecstatic about his resurrected life. Again Jesus said, "Peace be with you. As the Father has sent me, so I send you."

God wants peace in the hearts of individuals. If you are torn by inner conflict, Jesus is saying to you, "Peace be with you. My peace I give to you." If you are frustrated about bad relationships, Jesus wants you to have inner peace. If you are worried about your health, your job, or your children, Jesus says, "Peace be with you."

God knows turmoil is destructive to us. It causes stress, which makes us less effective and often brings illness. Family fights confuse children and warp their personalities. When chaos reigns within an individual, family or nation, God is not pleased, because God wants quiet order in life for his children. Healthy people also desire personal peace, which is like a precious jewel. Calm spirits also make for healthy marriages and wholesome families. Even work places are more productive when harmony prevails.

Inner peace comes through being at peace with God. Quietness comes when our hearts are free from guilt, and our lives free from destructive, enslaving habits. God loves us so much, God wants for us to have the best life, which is a life of peace. Paul wrote that living close to God will give us peace. "And the peace of God, which surpasses all understanding, will guard your hearts and your minds in Christ Jesus." (Philippians 4:7)

Drunkenness and drugs give people a false sense of peace. Turning our dependency from these destructive things to a dependency on God brings a genuine, natural peace. Working ourselves out of the rut of alcoholism is hard, but worth the real quietness of heart it brings.

Dear God, thank you so much for wanting me to have peace of heart. I praise you for caring that I have quietness of soul. Help me to allow you to bring this gift to me. In Jesus' name. Amen

Jesus wants me to have peace, and surely, I want it too.

Hope for Being a Peacemaker

"Blessed are the peacemakers, for they will be called children of God."
Matthew 5:9

Every decent and healthy human being wants peace. We want peace in our homes, our community, nation and world. God wants peace among people, which is why Jesus praised peacemakers in this beatitude.

There is hope in peace, and we hope that we can add peace to the world. If you and I are to be peacemakers, one of the practical requirements is humility. We must emulate Jesus, who humbled himself in order to bring peace. We see the difference humility made in his life. Before he was born Jesus was with God, and Jesus was God. Even though he was God, he humbled himself and gave that up in order to become a human. Throughout his life, Jesus practiced humility. Paul wrote that this humble spirit followed Jesus even to his death — "And being found in human form, he humbled himself and became obedient to the point of death—even death on a cross." (Philippians 2:7d-8) This amazing spirit brought peace to the world through healing and wholeness.

The humility shown by Jesus had eluded Adam and Eve, who as mere humans wanted to become like God. The snake in the garden promised them that if they ate of the forbidden tree of good and evil they would become their own gods no longer needing God. Through their pride-filled behavior they brought evil and disharmony into the world. Most of our problems in life come because we follow the Adam and Eve model. Although human, we want to be like God, and we act as though we were God. That sinful behavior is a recipe for the disharmony that emblazons the headlines of our newspapers.

When conflict arises, praying gives God the opportunity to give us peace. Through humbling ourselves before God, we receive insights into how to handle our relationships. Through prayer God quiets the inner heart, so the words and actions on the outside contribute to greater peace.

Christians at their best are peacemakers. Paul's letter to the churches of his day often reflected his concern for peace for them. He frequently wrote, "Grace to you and peace from God our Father and the Lord Jesus Christ."

ﻌﻟﻌﻟﻌﻟ

Thank you, God, for wanting peace in my world. I am grateful that you want me to help bring a "peace that passes all understanding." Give me grace to do what is in my power to make this happen in the world around me. In Jesus' name. Amen

Am I complainer or a fixer? A critic or a complimenter? Do I sow seeds of discord or seeds of peace?

Hope to be the Real Me

---

*"And God said, 'Let us make humankind in our image,
according to our likeness;" Genesis 1:26*

When God created you, you were given a basic personality, which is your essential self. That wonderful person resides in you as someone special, loved by God. However, we sometimes seem to lose touch with our real selves. Knowing who we really are and becoming who we want to be is one of the most difficult aspects of life.

A persona is a mask we put on to satisfy others. It is an outward layer of personality different than the one inside. Often it is uncomfortable living behind that mask, but we do it for security because we think that is what others expect of us. On a personal level, we are actors giving up our true personality taking on one that is not ours. A dear friend in his fifties said, "When I look in the mirror, I don't recognize myself any more."

Who am I? What is the true self within me? The true you is the one who was first in Adam and Eve before sin entered the world. When God created the world, he said, "Let us make humankind in our image, according to our likeness..." God made you with the qualities of God. Your most genuine self, the real self within you, is the most wonderful self that God first created all to be. Living closely with Jesus Christ allows the onion peel of false personality to be gently lifted from us, layer by layer, so we can become our true selves.

As you get in touch with that self, don't be afraid of it. Life is most wonderful when we are most completely in tune with ourselves and true to ourselves. There is no need to be fearful of ourselves because down inside there is the wonderful image of God.

While living close to God in prayer and fellowship within the church, God helps us get in touch with our true selves. When you invite Jesus into your heart, he will connect you with your own heart.

☙ ☙ ☙

Dear God, thank you so much for making me. I want to be a real person who is in touch with my deepest self. I invite Jesus into my heart and ask you to help me be the person you intended me to be. In Jesus' name. Amen

I want to be the most authentic person I can be.

Hope to Overcome Self-Centerness

*"Do nothing from selfish ambition or conceit, but in humility
regard others as better than yourselves." Philippians 2:3*

Amazing egotism dominates every generation. People focus on themselves and act out their lives from a self-centered view. They look at all of life mainly from a view of self.

It starts in childhood. Children who are not trained to think of others go through childhood very self-centered and later become self-centered teenagers who are a nightmare to their parents.

God did not make us self-centered. Cain didn't exhibit selfish behavior by killing his brother, Abel, until his parents had sinned. We were not created to focus primarily on self. Deep inside us is a loving heart that has great capacity to care for others. Underneath the crust of our false self-centeredness is a deeply loving person. At the core of our being, we have the capacity to care for others far more than you ever realized. Meanness is a shell covering up the real self. Down deep inside the mean person, there is grace and kindness. There is the loving spirit God created.

How do we overcome this self-centeredness to get in touch with who we really are?

How does the spirit of Christ get unraveled? How do we peel off our self-centeredness to get to the real, caring you and me? First, it is important to yield ourselves to Jesus Christ, accepting him as Savior and Lord. That basic act of humility immediately creates a new attitude of looking away from self. This includes honest self-examination and confession of sin. A new fundamental orientation takes place that is wonderfully liberating.

Then, as we walk the daily walk with Christ, we live as he did — a life of self-giving. Paul wrote, "Do nothing from selfish ambition or conceit..." Getting involved in helping others is fundamental. By giving ourselves, our minds move from thinking of self to thinking of others.

Power to overcome self is also wonderfully available through prayer. The shortest distance between your problems and their solutions is the distance between your knees and the floor. One of the most effective ways to cut the crusty layer of self-centeredness and selfishness away is to spend time humbly on your knees.

⚜ ⚜ ⚜

Loving God, thank you that at my deepest level I am like Christ, who came that he might help others. Enable me to help others, so I can be more concerned about them. In Jesus' name. Amen

I am happiest when my life is centered on loving God and others.

Day 20
Hope to have Hope

"Blessed be the God and Father of our Lord Jesus Christ!
By his great mercy he has given us a new birth into a living hope
through the resurrection of Jesus Christ from the dead..." I Peter 1:3

Sometimes life can be so heavy, that it's hard to hope. It is difficult to believe there is a way out. By God's mercy, we can have hope in all things. No day is ever so dark that Christians cannot see the light of hope. No situation is ever so complex that God does not show us a way out. Trusting in God always gives us hope. Opening our lives to God's grace infuses us with confidence to say, "We are going to get through this."

When the angel announced to Mary that she would become pregnant, Mary asked, "How can this be, since I am a virgin? The angel said to her, 'The Holy Spirit will come upon you, and the power of the most High will overshadow you; therefore the child to be born will be holy; he will be called Son of God...For nothing will be impossible with God."(Luke 1:34b,35,37) Just as Mary was assured of possibilities beyond her dreams, they also exist for you. God has amazing power to help you with your daily problems beyond your imagination. You can have great hope.

Years ago, when cruel Apartheid was the rule in South Africa, the government devised a plan to destroy Mogopa, a village west of Johannesburg. Its inhabitants were to be removed forcibly at gunpoint and moved to another area. On the eve of their departure, the village clinics, shops, schools and churches had already been demolished. That evening, church leaders from all over South Africa held a vigil at Mogopa. Around mid night, an elder of the doomed village got up to pray. Desmond Tutu was there and reports that it was the strangest prayer he ever heard and one he will never forget. The old man about ready to lose his home and see his village destroyed, prayed, "God, thank you for loving us so much." That was not only a prayer of love but of hope. Now, several years later, Apartheid is dead, and the people of Mogopa have returned and are rebuilding their village. God, indeed, loved those people and gave them hope that did not forsake them.

ريا ريا ريا

God of hope, inspire hope within me today. Help me to see possibilities where none appear. Open my eyes to see doors of opportunity where the future seems to be a huge wall. In Jesus' name. Amen

I will believe the angel's words, that nothing is impossible with God for me.

Hope to Overcome Self Doubt

"I can do all things through…(Christ) him, who strengthens me."
Philippians 4:13

The apostle Paul wrote these words in the context of difficult circumstances, which could have engendered self-doubt. He had experiences of Jesus Christ empowering him when he was weak and had little strength. He writes that the power of God can embolden us when the uneasiness of doubt begins to buckle our knees. Self-doubt is not from God and need not cripple us

Self-doubt can trigger various false ways of overcoming it. One is liquor. Drinking liquor to excess releases one from inhibitions, thus giving a person an unreal sense of confidence. An alcoholic was visiting with his pastor when he said, "Unless I have a drink I am going to die." It was evening, and the pastor said, "Why don't you go home and die." The man did—he went home and died to his false self. It was his false self that told him he could not handle life without escaping to the bottle. He was afraid he couldn't handle life and covered up his self-doubt leaning on the crutch of liquor. His inhibitions were minimized by every drink he had. When that old self-doubt died, he realized he could indeed handle life without getting soused. Then he got in touch with his real self, which gave him confidence to tackle daily problems in a healthy manner.

God did not make you and me to be self-doubting people. God meant for us to have freedom, strength and joy. Down inside you there is a confident person who says with the apostle Paul, "I can do all things through …(Christ), which strengthens me."

Teenagers sometimes are burdened with self-doubts about their intelligence or physical appearance. Their parents may hear them say, "I am dumb," or "I am ugly." Upon hearing such words, wise parents will lovingly say, "In this house, you are not allowed to put yourself down." Then the parents will do all they can to love and affirm that child.

When you doubt yourself about anything, God wants to hear about it. Just as every earthly parent wants his or her child full of confidence, God wants you, his earthly child, to have no self-doubts. Therefore, you can bring your self-concerns to God in prayer. "And this is the boldness we have in him, that if we ask anything according to his will, he hears us." (I John 5:14)

❧ ❧ ❧

Dear God, thank you that I am precious in your eyes. Where I doubt myself help me to open myself to your strength. Give me confidence so that I can handle every situation I face today by the power of your Holy Spirit. In Jesus' name. Amen

With God's help, I will have victory in everything I do today.

Day 22

Hope in Prayers of Praise

"Praise the Lord! Praise the name of the Lord; give praise,
O servants of the Lord..." Psalm 135:1

The highest form of prayer is praise because it is totally devoid of self-centeredness or selfishness. Praise does not think of self but arises simply for who and what God is. It is higher than thanksgiving because even thanksgiving considers the self. In thanksgiving we ponder what God has done for us, but in praise we consider only the wonder and glory of God.

There is hope in praise because praise takes our minds off our own problems and centers them on the greatness and wonder of God. Therein lies the hope for all of humanity and the answer to all human need. Praise frees the spirit and lifts our hope to a higher level. The darkness of hopelessness comes when persons wallow in their own needs and pains. The sunlight of hope shines brightly upon us when we see the greatness and glory of God. Hopelessness comes from seeing only our problems, but praise brings hope because it turns our eyes to the source of our solutions.

Hope exudes from joining with the Psalmist, who wrote, "Bless the Lord, O my soul, O Lord my God, you are very great. You are clothed with honor and majesty, wrapped in light as with a garment. You stretch out the heavens like a tent." (Psalms 104:1-2) Being children of such a great God gives us enormous hope.

Praise is hard. It requires forgetting about ourselves and centering only on the greatness of God. But if we can grow to lifting our thoughts and voices to tell God how great we think God is, that will fill us with hope. Praise of God enlivens our hope because it fills our hearts and minds with God, who is the answer to all our questions and the solution to all of our problems.

To some it may appear as escapism, but praise is a beautiful and sweet form of hope. We receive hope centering on the glory, the power and the wonder of God.

Dear God, I praise you for who you are. My heart rejoices because of your glory and greatness. When I ponder your beauty and majesty, my problems seem to disappear into nothing. I rejoice that you are a wonderful God. In Jesus' name. Amen

Praising God puts all of life in a new perspective of hope.

Hope in Prayers of Thanksgiving

"As you therefore have received Christ Jesus the Lord, continue to live your lives in him, rooted and built up in him and established in the faith, just as you were taught, abounding in thanksgiving." Colossians 2:6-7

If you spend time thanking God every day for your blessings, God will bring deeper and renewed hope into your life. List ten things every day for which you are grateful, and God will open your eyes to greater promise for your life. Seeing how faithful God is to you now will inspire hope for God's continued faithfulness in the future. God told Moses to annually remember the Passover, when God spared the first born of Israel from death in Egypt. This yearly reminder helps the faithful of Israel know what God has done in the past, and is the basis of hope for what God can do now and in the future.

Daily remembering our blessings and thanking God for them, fills us with joy. Ending the day with prayers of thanksgiving gives us a quiet reminder of how our hope was fulfilled that day. God does not disappoint our hope. Beginning the day with gratitude for the night of rest, for a refreshed spirit and renewed mind, gives hope for the wonderful prospect of a new day. It is a whole clean slate of new hours from God for us to fill. That is a great basis for daily hope.

A heart grateful to God is a heart hopeful for God to do new things. Gratitude inspires hope. The person who has experienced the great works of Jesus Christ in the past moves forward with expectation that God will do the same wonderful things in the future.

When you live a thankful life, it fills the people around you with greater hope. Thankful people are a ray of sunshine in a world darkened with disappointment. The thankful person in a household brings smiles to a family, which undergird the optimism of hope.

A basic virtue of the Christian faith is gratitude. The apostle Paul wrote to the Christians in Philippi, "Do not worry about anything, but in everything by prayer and supplication with thanksgiving let your requests be made known to God." (Philippians 4:6) Praying with a thankful heart brings hope.

Dear and faithful God, thank you for taking care of me throughout my life. I thank you for this new day and for the anticipation of your continued goodness. Fill my life with hope that you will do your wonderful work in and through me this day. In Jesus' name. Amen

I want to be a profoundly thankful person for all of God's goodness.

Hope Through Confession

"If we confess our sins, he who is faithful and just will forgive us our sins and cleanse us from all unrighteousness." I John 1:9

The basis for Christian confession is God's coming to us in Jesus Christ while making a new covenant with us. God allowed Jesus to die, so we can have new beginnings through being forgiven for our sins. Jesus told Nicodemus it is a "born again" experience — a coming to new life. Paul had that new birth experience with Jesus Christ, when his life was dramatically altered. He was transformed from an enemy of Jesus Christ to one of his most ardent supporters and staunch workers. God is the God of new beginnings, which gives us hope.

When we confess our sins God forgives us, and we have a new, clean slate — a fresh start that enlivens us with hope. Confession and forgiveness turn our eyes away from an enslaving past to a freeing future. The weight of the old guilt is lifted and we are freed to move into a glorious future unburdened by our previous sins. Excitedly, we move forward with new and joyous expectations.

Guilt is an enormous burden. It twists the mind and weakens the spirit. King David felt this weight upon his heart when the prophet Nathan challenged him. David had sinned terribly in his affair with Bathsheba, not only in committing sexual sin, but also in having Bathsheba's fine husband, Uriah, murdered. The king had tried to cover up this despicable behavior, but the prophet exposed him. After David responded, "I have sinned against the Lord." (2 Samuel 12:13) he felt a burden removed from his shoulders and received new hope.

The apostle Paul linked confession of sin and new life in Christ to being reconciled with God. Being reconnected with our Creator gives us daily and profound hope. The power God used to create the universe is available to conquer our human weakness. This is hope to the highest degree.

Through confession and forgiveness we see life with new eyes. People once seen as objects to be used are seen as children of God. While sinful behavior once looked so appealing, we are now appalled by it. Instead of flirting with it, we flee from it. Herein is a new kind of hope.

ele ele ele

God of new beginnings, thank you for the grace to confess my sins and to ask your pardon. We are grateful you have taken our sins upon yourself and set us free. This gives us enormous hope to live our lives with confidence. In Jesus' name. Amen

I want the hope that comes through daily confession and forgiveness.

Day 25

Hope Through Intercession

"In our prayers for you we always thank God, the Father of our
Lord Jesus Christ," Colossians 1:3

With these words, the apostle Paul was telling the Christians in the city of Colossae that he prayed for them. Such words fill the pages of the New Testament. The early Christians believed in praying for others because they knew God provided hope through such prayers.

It is a great gift to intercede for others. Lifting loved ones, friends, neighbors and strangers to God in prayer is a wonderful act of mercy. It brings hope to those for whom we pray. Documented studies on prayer show how God brought special healing to those lifted up to God in prayer.

God invites us to pray for others. This gives us hope to help them in a unique way. Through prayer, God blesses people in other parts of the country and world when we otherwise could do nothing.

Through praying for others, God not only blesses the ones we pray for, but God also changes us. One of the gentlest ways by which God peels away selfishness and self-centeredness is through praying for others. If you want to grow into a more loving person, begin praying for others. The Holy Spirit will lovingly transform you into a more caring person. Pray that God will sincerely bless others, and in the process God will give you special grace as well. While earnestly praying for others, we provide hope for them and for ourselves.

Jesus said we ought also to pray for our enemies. Now that takes special grace! He said, "But I say to you, love your enemies and pray for those who persecute you..." (Matthew 5:44) When we pray for those who make life difficult for us, not only are they blessed, but we are also transformed. God makes us bigger, more gracious and loving people. That enables God to use us more effectively in daily life.

⚜ ⚜ ⚜

Dear God, thank you for the great gift of intercession. It is a privilege to pray for others, knowing that you minister to them through our prayers bringing them new hope. I am grateful that while lifting others to be blessed, you also bless me. In Jesus' name. Amen

When God invites us to pray for others, one of the greatest gifts is given to us.

Day 26

Hope in God's Protection

We are "being protected by the power of God through faith for a salvation ready to be revealed in the last time." I Peter 1:5

The early Christians lived in peril, as they were persecuted for their faith in Jesus Christ. However, they believed that in their danger, the power of God was protecting them. Peter expressed this faith, when he wrote we are "being protected by the power of God." As we walk by faith in Jesus Christ, God looks after us. As we seek to do God's will in every moment of our lives, God puts a fence of protection around us. As we focus on God's will, God takes care of us. In our hope we are surrounded by the power of God.

Peter knew the story of Israel as God led them out of enslavement to Egypt. As the people were about to cross the Red Sea into freedom, they could hear the thundering hoofs of horses pulling hundreds of Pharaoh's chariots. Pharaoh was coming to recapture the people of Israel. The Israelites cringed and froze with fear, but Moses said to them, "Do not be afraid, stand firm, and see the deliverance of the Lord will accomplish for you today; for the Egyptians whom you see today you shall never see again. The Lord will fight for you, and you have only to keep still." The people of Israel did trust God, and they were delivered from the hands of Pharaoh. God fought their battle for them.

When teenaged David clad only in shepherd's clothes faced the giant Goliath covered with armor, he said to Goliath, "This very day the Lord will deliver you into my hand...for the battle is the Lord's and he will give you into our hand." (I Samuel 17:46a & 47b) David knew the fight was lost if it depended only on his strength, but when protected by God, victory was assured.

While trusting God, God fights our battles for us. Yes, we are also involved, but the power of God is the force that will bring us victory. Herein lies our hope.

Knowing the protective power of God gives us hope. Putting our faith in Jesus Christ, God puts a hedge of security around us. We are protected from many things that would hurt us. When open to God's direction, the Holy Spirit guides us away from harm.

Almighty God, thank you for your power and for making it available to me. I praise you for protecting me, and putting a fence of safety around my life. Help me to open myself to your power. In Jesus' name. Amen

Today I want to trust in the power of God for whatever issues I face in my life.

Day 27

Hope in God's Removing Obstacles

"When they looked up, they saw that the stone, which was very large, had already been rolled back." Mark 16:4

On the first Easter morning Mary Magdalene, Salome and Mary the mother of James went to the tomb early in the morning. As they walked along "They had been saying to one another, 'Who will roll away the stone for us from the entrance to the tomb?'" This rock was far too heavy for 3 women to remove. Their worry was unnecessary, because when they got there the stone had already been rolled away. God had anticipated their coming and had removed the obstacle that would keep them out of Jesus' tomb.

We all have rock like obstacles keeping us from achieving goals. Some struggle against the rock of unemployment or underemployment. Others feel blocked from their goals of bringing harmony into their families. Some fight the huge rock of undiscipline keeping them from overcoming a destructive habit of liquor, sex or drugs. Still others have found hostility a rock that blocks intimate relationships and even physical health. All sometimes feel they are dragging a rock of inertia, which keeps them from fulfilling objectives and goals. These rocks seem to have been placed in our paths by forces bigger than we are, and we are not strong enough to move them. It may not remove our rocks, but it is good to know that everybody has some boulders in their lives obstructing them.

If you hold animosity or hatred in your heart today, let God roll that stone away. It is blocking your path to a happier life for yourself, to good relationships with your family and even to a healthier life. Jesus Christ can roll that stone away from your life. Jesus Christ can set you free. As we put our faith in Jesus Christ, rock like obstacles are indeed removed for us by God.

God removed the rock from the tomb that first Easter morning without any human help. Although God still causes quakes that move rocks today, God usually needs your help. If you work with God, virtually every rock like obstacle can be removed from your life.

❧ ❧ ❧

Dear God, thank you for wanting to remove barricades from my life. I praise you for your power to do that. Help me to trust in your rock moving power, and to work with you in your efforts. In Jesus' name. Amen

Am I willing to let God remove obstacles from my life? Or, do I prefer to have them there as an excuse for my not succeeding?

Hope Through Other People

"They devoted themselves to the apostle's teaching and fellowship, to the breaking of bread and to prayer." Acts 2:42

God created the church on Pentecost with three thousand new people becoming followers of Christ. After that magnificent event, those early Christians spent time together in teaching, fellowship, worship and prayer. Great things happen, when God's people meet in harmony. God uses other people to enrich our lives, and help us become far more than we could ever become alone. Jesus came to the disciples on the first Easter, when they were gathered together. God usually enables us to grow and become our best selves in association with other people.

In every metropolitan, suburban, small town and rural area of America, there is much loneliness. With people all around them, many feel very much alone. Loneliness keeps them from finding joy, peace, strength and success.

Loneliness even affects our health. A study was made of a group exposed to a cold virus to see who would start coughing. Those involved in a family, church or club were the least likely to get sick. Having six or more such ties gave a person the best chance to fight illness. The loners with 3 or 4 fewer relationships had a four times higher chance of succumbing to the cold virus. Loneliness can even cause death. Through fellowship with others in our families and at church God helps us overcome loneliness, which helps us remain alive and healthy.

One way God helps us through friendships is that they enable us to know ourselves. This truly is a short life, and its brevity makes it urgent that we get to know ourselves. Dostoyesky said it is a tragedy that so many people never find themselves. They do not know who they are, and that is an important reason for friendships. Friends are mirrors, who help us see who we really are. Our conversations with them reflect back to us what they are seeing and hearing. And God can help us deal with life more effectively, when we know who we are.

❧ ❧ ❧

Dear God, thank you for friends and loved ones, who make life so much more enjoyable. Thank you for the caring, encouragement and learning we gain through others. Help me to be open to your blessings as they come through others. In Jesus' name. Amen

I will open my life to others, who care for me.

Hope for Our Resurrection

"Now if Christ is proclaimed as raised from the dead, how can some of you say there is no resurrection of the dead?" I Corinthians 15:12

In every age people have asked what happens to us after death. People in the early church said, "If Jesus is was raised from the dead, will that really happen to us as well. Will we be raised from the dead just as he was?" The Apostle Paul answered the question with a question, "Now if Christ is proclaimed as raised from the dead, how can some of you say there is no resurrection of the dead? If there is no resurrection of the dead, then Christ has not been raised..." In other words, if God raised Christ from the dead then he will also raise you. In Paul's words, "If for this life only we have hoped in Christ, we are of all people most to be pitied." (I Cor. 15:19)

Paul wrote if we are not raised, then we do not have to be concerned with how we live. If a shovel of dirt on our coffins ends our existence, Paul writes, "Let us eat and drink for tomorrow we die." (I Cor. 15:32) If there is no resurrection and no judgment from God, let's make life a big party, and get the most out of it just for us.

Indeed, we will have a glorious life with God in heaven, so if we put our trust in Jesus Christ, there is nothing to fear. God will welcome us to that Great Beyond the rainbow with open arms saying, "Well done, thou good and faithful servant." Walking with Jesus in this life gives us the best life this world has to offer, and we have the wonderful hope for the world to come. We cannot explain how God is able to bring new life, but we live convinced that the dead are raised.

Live in that glorious hope and say with Paul, "Death has been swallowed up in victory. Where, O death, is your victory? Where, O Death, is your sting?...But thanks be to God, who gives us the victory through our Lord Jesus Christ."

ﻋﻠﻰ ﻋﻠﻰ ﻋﻠﻰ

Dear God, we thank you so much for hope of life beyond this life. I am grateful for an exciting time when I will see God "face to face", and I will be with my loved ones and all the saints of old. In Jesus' name. Amen

A great, glorious life awaits me in the next world.

Hope for Overcoming Bad Habits

"You were taught to put away your former way of life, your old self, corrupt and deluded by its lusts, and to be renewed in the spirit of your minds, and to clothe yourselves with the new self, created according to the likeness of God in true righteousness and holiness." Ephesians 4:22-24

All sincere Christians want to live the best lives they can, but all bring baggage of regret as they begin their walk with Christ. We want to honor God with our minds, our mouths and our behavior. But how do we do it?

Paul reminded the Christians in Ephesus, that they were taught to get rid of sinful behavior from their former lives. They needed to move away from their previous ways, which were "corrupt and deluded by its lusts." But, how were they to do that?

By being "renewed in the spirit of your minds" and by being reclothed with new selves. By trusting in Jesus Christ, they were to allow him to remold their lives. Consequently, people dead in destructive habits were given new life. The hopeless and depressed filled with despair were raised to new life of peace and joy, as they put their deep and sincere trust in Jesus Christ. Frustrated husbands and wives with marriages nearly in the coffin found God raising their relationship to new life. The sick whose bodies had been stricken with ailments were healed. Some without purpose standing at dead end alleys were directed to open highways of life filled with new meaning and excitement. The Ephesian Christians began believing the angel, who said to Mary at the birth of Jesus, "For nothing is impossible with God."

Christians, by trusting in Jesus Christ see God bring new life to people constantly. Spending time in prayer to God, we open our hearts and minds to God's holy influence. By reading and studying God's word, hateful and negative thought patterns are made loving and hopeful. God's way of overcoming bad behavior is to replace it with good, and it happens as your daily walk with Christ draws you closer to him.

Dear Jesus, thank you for helping me to become like you. I am grateful for loving thoughts replacing hateful ones, and for self-giving replacing my greedy tendencies. Lord, remold me into a wonderful, godly person. In your name. Amen

I want my whole being to become more Christ like.

Hope Through Grace

"For by grace you have been saved through faith, and this is not your own doing; it is a gift of God—." Ephesians 2:8

All of life indeed is a gift. Life is full of kindness, goodness and mercy. We receive it all the time, and don't fully understand it. Do you think you are not receiving grace? Think about this. You are receiving grace from God and are totally unaware of it. For example, right now God is giving your heart life, so it is beating nearly 4000 times every hour. What are you doing to make that possible? Your only contribution is breathing. The heart beating in your body is a gift from God.

We live grace even though it can't be put into a test tube. How do you explain a parent giving herself or himself endlessly for a child who is rebellious and no longer deserving of kindness? How do you explain a loving wife sticking with a drunken husband or a loving husband putting up with an alcoholic wife? How do you explain a child continuing to love a parent, who abused him or her?

God has a storehouse of grace for you that has hardly been tapped. God has goodness to share with you beyond your imagination. By opening yourself to God daily through prayer, mercy and kindness will fill your life. Through reading scripture the Holy Spirit infuses our spirits with goodness. As we lay down our lives on behalf of others, we receive mercy. Grace comes to us also by sharing in fellowship with other believers. God wants a better life for you than you want for yourself.

It is not surprising that one of the best known and most favorite of hymns in America is Amazing Grace. It tells of the sweetness of God's goodness. It is grace that relieves our fears, and helps us through difficult times. This divine mercy promises good to us and secures us with hope.

When people allow the risen Christ to fill their hearts and minds, they receive grace to share grace. If you want grace, meet the Christ of grace. Grow in Christ, and you will receive grace, which will flow through you to others.

❦ ❦ ❦

God of grace, thank you for your kindness to me. I praise your name for the mercy you share even when I am undeserving. Help me to learn new ways every day to let your grace to enter my life and to flow through me to others. In Jesus' name. Amen

God has amazing grace to share with me today.

Day 32

Hope by Forgiving Others

"...be kind to one another, tenderhearted, forgiving one another,
as God in Christ has forgiven you." Ephesians 4:32

A life of anger and vengeance is a life without hope. There is hope only in forgiveness.

There are two great stories of forgiveness in the Bible. The first is Jesus hanging on the cross. He was an innocent man, who had committed no crime. He had lived a life without sin, and was nailed to the cross blameless before God. His body was suspended on that cross only with nails holding his wrists and feet to the wood. He was writhing with pain under the hot Mediterranean sun. Looking down at those who nailed him there, those causing his death, he prayed to God, "Father, forgiven them; for they do not know what they are doing."

The second story is of the early Christian, Stephen. He was being stoned to death, because he preached about Jesus Christ. As the hateful men were throwing stones at his face and body, he was hurting terribly. Rocks hurled at his face tore his skin causing blood to run down his checks. Rock after rock kept coming without interruption. There was nobody to defend him. He stood alone. Finally as the stones began crushing his skull, Stephen began losing it. Looking at his murderers as his body was crumbling in death, he prayed, "Lord, do not hold this sin against them."

Forgiving those who hurt us brings hope. There is hope, because forgiveness brings life. Holding on to anger and bitterness destroys us. It saps our energy, distracts our minds and thus makes us less effective. God graciously forgives us, and thereby gives us new hope. When we forgive others, we receive new hope because we are made free.

The apostle Paul had ample reason to be angry with his persecutors. He had been beaten and pursued by mobs for his faith in Jesus Christ. Of his persecution in Asia he wrote, "Indeed, we felt that we had received the sentence of death..." (I Cor. 1:9a)

But, instead of seeking revenge on his enemies, he preached love. Indeed, he wrote to the Roman Christians, "Beloved, never avenge yourselves, but leave room for the wrath of God; for it is written, 'Vengeance is mine, I will repay, says the Lord.'" (Rom. 12:19)

❧ ❧ ❧ ❧

Dear God, thank you for giving me hope when I forgive others. I am grateful for grace to forgive, and for the wonderful freedom that you give. In Jesus' name. Amen

I receive new hope and life, when I forgive others. Whom I have not forgiven?

Hope in Loving God

"(Jesus) said to him, 'You shall love the Lord your God with all your heart, and with all your soul, and with all your mind.'" Matthew 22:37

Jesus said loving God is our first priority in living. Loving God above all else gives us hope. Nothing else matters more. Hope comes because we know what is central to life. A feeling of security fills our hearts, when we know our mission in life. It is God's will for us to love God with all that we are.

And, there is hope in living in the center of that will. Loving God with our whole being puts us in the ultimate place of God's desire. We live in glorious light, when we give ourselves totally in loving God, which means doing God's bidding in all things. Hence, loving God puts us in the safest place in life.

Years ago our son, Paul, was traveling in Columbia, South America with a Christian music group. Travel in that drug troubled land was dangerous, and the group had to be escorted by armed guards as they passed through city airports with their instruments and sound equipment. Walking surrounded by men with automatic rifles was both relieving and unsettling to the young Christian musicians. It was calming to the group as they considered this thought, "The safest place for us to be is in the center of God's will."

Loving God is living in the center of God's will, and thus gives us wonderful hope. It is hope that fills our hearts with peace. It is hope, because it sustains us in our daily living. In our loving God more than anything else, we are gloriously supported by God. God is on our side; and by loving God with all our being, we live in the heart of God. It is a place of light and contentment.

I recommend you consider making this little prayer a major part of your daily life: "Dear God, I love you. Lord Jesus Christ, I love you. Holy Spirit God, I love you." Praying these endearing words brings peace to the heart and sweetness to the soul.

Dear God, thank you for helping us understand our first mission is to love you with all our being. We are grateful for grace to center ourselves totally on you, and we praise you for the hope, peace and joy that we have in doing so. In Jesus' name. Amen

I want to love God today and every day with all that I am.

Hope Through God's Love for us

"For God so loved the world, that he gave his own son, that whoever believes in him will not perish but may have eternal life." John 3:16

Our ultimate hope comes from knowing we are loved by the God of the universe. If the God, who created the billions of galaxies each with its billion stars, loves you very deeply, what else matters? Nothing is more important.

This wonderfully loving God loved you so much, that he came to earth in the human form, we would call Jesus. God did this to take our sins and failures upon himself, so we can be free from guilt to live this life to the hilt.

John wrote in his first letter, "God is love, and those who abide in love abide in God, and God abides in them." All the caring in the world originates in and continues by God. The wonder and goodness of humanity was grown through the garden of God's sprouting blessings.

The glory of compassionate outreach began with God's loving creation of Adam and Eve.

God made you to have a child to love. God sustains us with daily breath and keeps our hearts going with 4000 beats per hour, because God loves us so deeply. God made us to have children to care for, and as a mother lovingly nurtures an infant at her breast, God nurtures us daily with life. As a father joyously romps with his children in play, so God is with us daily to fill us with childlike joy.

You were made to be loved, so love is the essence of life, and it comes from our gracious God. All of the negatives of life are eclipsed by the positive and ever flowing love of God. The darkness of hate cannot remain dark in the light of God's brilliant loving kindness.

Because of God's love, God is in the redeeming business. He constantly wants to make things new. Therefore Jesus said, "Indeed, God did not send the Son into the world to condemn the world, but in order that the world might be saved through him."

❧ ❧ ❧

Loving God, thank you so much for your love for me. Help me to feel it deep within my heart and inside the marrow of my bones. May every fiber of my body feel the tender pulse of your love. In Jesus' name. Amen

I am completely and totally loved by the God who gives the sun its brilliance, the moon its glow and the stars their twinkle.

Day 35

Hope Through Loving People

"Beloved, let us love one another, because love is from God; everyone who loves is born of God and knows God. Whoever does not love does not know God, for God is love." I John 4:7-8

As God made you as a child for God to love, so God made others for us to love. Therein lies hope. A world without caring is a world without hope.

Loving people means wanting the best for them, and this love is not motivated by emotion but rather intention. To love our husbands, wives, children, parents and siblings is not dependent on our having strong positive feelings, but rather our desire to help them. Therein lies hope. We can do the best for others, even when we are not on an emotional high for them. We can control our loving, because it is motivated by intent. Whereas we are often at the mercy of our emotions, we control our intentions. We can love even when we don't feel like it; that is wonderfully hopeful.

Loving others brings hope to them. Our affirming people lifts their spirit, and puts a new bounce in their step. When others experience our love it lifts their eyes to the future with joyous anticipation removing their fixations on past failures and pains. That instills hope.

But loving others is not only a blessing for them, it brings us deep satisfaction as well.

Jesus said we are blessed, when we lose ourselves on behalf of others. We find life in doing that. On the other hand, we lose our lives, when we use our energies and gifts just for ourselves. While giving our lives for others is a great blessing for them, it simultaneously deepens our lives with joy and contentment. As we bring hope to others, we find new hope ourselves.

John wrote, "…if we love one another, God lives in us, and his love is perfected in us." (I John 4:12 b,c) God's living in us brings a peace that passes all understanding. Jesus lives in our hearts, when we love one another.

ﺯﻟ ﺯﻟ ﺯﻟ

Dear God, thank you that I can be a loving person, whose love is not dependent upon my feelings, but my desire to want the best for everyone. Give me this wonderful grace most deeply. In Jesus' name. Amen

I want to be the most loving person I can be.

Hope Through Companionship

---

*"When he was at the table with them, he took bread, blessed and broke it,
and gave it to them. Then their eyes were opened, and they recognized him..."*
Luke 24:30-31a,b,

The Latin word, *com*, means "with," and the Latin word, *panis*, means "bread."
Those two words are the roots for our English word, companion, which literally means, "with bread." A companion originally was a meal mate with whom
you ate. Today a companion is someone you spend time with doing anything.

God blesses our lives with hope, when we enter companionship with others.
On the first Easter two of Jesus' disciples walked toward their home in Emmaus
dejected. They had been in Jerusalem, where Jesus had been crucified, and they
were despondent, because the one in whom they had put their trust was now
dead.

The risen Christ joined them as they walked, but they did not recognize him.
When they shared their pain, he gave them understanding they did not have. He
told them how the prophets and all of their scriptures told exactly what had
happened to Jesus. They learned from him.

When they reached Emmaus they turned to go to their home, but this stranger
appeared to be continuing. As it was evening, the disciples invited him to spend
the night. After preparing a meal, they sat down to eat, and it was in the breaking
of bread they recognized the stranger was their beloved Jesus. Their hope was
revived, and they immediately got up and returned to Jerusalem to meet the other
disciples.

Living alone can be very lonely taking away our zest for life. Finding companionship lifts the spirit, and renews hope. We gain new understanding of life, when
we talk about it with others. It sharpens our perspective, and often brings joy
and laughter. After Jesus' identity was made known to the two disciples, he disappeared. They then said to each other, "Were not our hearts burning within us
while he was talking to us on the road, while he was opening the scriptures to
us?" That brief time of companionship with Jesus rekindled their hope, and their
hearts were deeply touched.

It is amazing how God comes to us, when we allow ourselves the blessing of
Christian companionship.

*Dear God, thank you that Jesus said, "where two or three are gathered in my
name, there I am in the midst of them." I am grateful for the privilege of having
loved ones and friends, whose companionship gives me hope. In Jesus' name. Amen*

**I want to open my life to fellowship with others, so God can strengthen
my hope.**

Hope by Inviting Others Into Our Lives

"When he saw them, he ran from the tent entrance to meet them, and bowed down to the ground. He said, 'My lord, if I find favor with you, do not pass by your servant.'" Genesis 18:2b,3

This story from the eighteenth chapter of Genesis tells of an incident, when Abraham and Sarah were living on a farm isolated from others. Abraham was sitting at the entrance of his tent about noon, when he saw three men passing by his property. He ran to meet them, bowed before them, and then he said, "My lord, if I find favor with you, do not pass by your servant. Let a little water be brought, and wash your feet, and rest yourselves under the tree. Let me bring a little bread, that you may refresh yourselves, and after that you may pass on—since you have come to your servant."

Abraham offered them a meal, and while they were waiting for the big dinner to be prepared, the strangers told Abraham his wife was going to have a baby. Sarah and Abraham had waited decades for the child God had promised to them, and now God used total strangers to tell them about their baby to come. God comes to us with hope, when we open our lives to others.

Allowing others into our lives brings the hope of overcoming not only loneliness, but also limitation. Shutting others out of our lives deprives us of new and deeper perspectives of life, which would enrich us in a wonderful way. Allowing them into our midst can give us new understandings making our lives more effective. We become more than we otherwise would be, when we open ourselves to others.

God was in the three visitors bringing new hope to the tent of Abraham and Sarah. But God was only able to bring that hope, because Abraham was open to inviting them into his and Sarah's life. Many times God has the right people to come into our lives, but they come only as we are open to receive them. There is hope in opening our lives to others.

అంబా అంబా అంబా

Dear God, thank you for people, who love me and are very willing to come into my life bringing new hope. Give me grace to be vulnerable to invite them. In Jesus' name. Amen

I want that extra zest in life that others can bring as I invite them.

Hope in Being Known by Jesus

"I am the good shepherd. I know my own and my own know me,
just as the Father knows me and I know the Father." John 10:14-15a

It is wonderful to be known. I have called homes, when children answered the telephone simply saying, "hello." Then when I said their names, I could hear them tell their mothers in the background, "He knows my name." Stories are told of sales people going into hotels where they had not been for months, and they were utterly impressed because the attendent behind the registration desk called them by name. We love to hear our names.

In an impersonal world there is hope in being known. Jesus said, "I am the good shepherd. I know my own and my own know me, just as the Father knows me and I know the Father." Jesus and God were close, and knew each other well. But Jesus the shepherd of people also knows his flock. He knows his sheep by name. Through Isaiah, the prophet, God said, "...it is I the God of Israel, who call you by your name." (45:3c) The shepherd knows his sheep well.

I am constantly amazed at how some people can identify your voice without caller ID before you say your name. Usually, I assume that no one knows my voice on the phone, so I always introduce myself. It is embarrassing when people telephone and assume you know their voice, and then you finally have to ask, "With whom am I speaking?" When praying to Jesus, our good shepherd, we never need to give our names. Jesus the good shepherd not only knows us by name but also by voice. He even knows the thoughts we are thinking, and what attitudes we have in our hearts.

To be known on a human level is to have an intimate relationship, and to be known by Jesus is the ultimate intimacy. Sometimes we shy away from intimacy, because we do not know if we can trust the person. We can open up completely to our Good Shepherd, because he is completely trustworthy. His love for us is unconditional, and there is hope in the fact that he knows you.

Dear Jesus, thank you for being my Good Shepherd, who knows me completely. It gives me hope to know someone cares for me so much to want to know me so well. In your name. Amen

I love to be known, and it is particularly wonderful to be known by Jesus.

Day 39

Hope Through Being A New Person

"You have been born anew, not of perishable seed but of imperishable seed, through the living and enduring word of God." I Peter 1:23

He would have been the dream of every American family. A highly intelligent child, who was reading about calculus at the age of 10. In high school he was one of the brightest kids in his class getting some of the highest grades. Before he got his driver's license at the age of 16, he was off to Harvard University. He got his masters and Ph. D. from the University of Michigan. His Ph. D. dissertation solved a math problem his professor could not do. Doesn't every family dream of having a child and successful youth like this? A child of tremendous intelligence and magnificent educational achievement?

Americans now know the man described as the Unabomber, who held our land at bay for nearly 18 yrs. He is believed to have mailed highly sophisticated explosive packages and letters that killed 3 and injured 23. Millions of dollars were spent to cover the damage of his work and to track him down. This man had two of the possessions most highly prized by Americans, great intelligence and much education. This story shows that these two assets without God can be highly destructive. In fact, the greater the intelligence and education, the greater the potential for evil in a godless person. The message for America is that along with intelligence and education we need to put God into the hearts of our people. We need what the Bible calls being born again.

There is great hope in finding new life in Christ. We find a new future of letting God take control of our lives. Peter wrote, "You have been born anew, not of perishable but of imperishable seed, through the living and enduring word of God." The term, born anew or born again, as the King James Version puts it, describes the process of becoming a Christian. The Christian is someone who is twice born. The first time physically and the second time spiritually.

When we find new life in Jesus Christ, our depressive self-centeredness is shed for a refreshing and glorious God centeredness. Herein is great hope.

✥ ✥ ✥

Dear God, thank you for grace to become new persons. What a blessing to find that clean, unburdened life in you. I am grateful for the hope of new life in Jesus Christ. In his name. Amen

I want the gift of a cleansing and freeing new birth in Jesus Christ.

New Hope Through Over Coming Self

"I have been crucified with Christ; and it is no longer I who live, but it is Christ who lives in me. And the life I now live in the flesh I live by faith in the Son of God, who loved me and gave himself for me." Galatians 2:19b-20

There is wonderful hope that comes through Jesus Christ by whom we can conquer our egos. The self can be exceedingly damaging to us. Our egos can trip us up enormously causing conflict in relationships, bad decisions and wasted life. Egos not under control can bring great heartbreak, emotional imbalance, ill health and even death.

Ego problems begin at birth. Every baby is centered on self, and that is the way of God. Unless a baby lets mom and dad know when it is hungry, mom and dad have no idea when to feed it. A wet diaper cry is helpful, because it alerts mom and dad to change it. When the baby hurts somewhere, it is necessary to hear a cry, otherwise healing attention would not come. God's plan is for babies to be self-centered and to get the attention they need in order to become healthy, happy and strong children.

But God's plan is for that same baby as a child or youth to have its will redirected away from self toward God. The control seat of every human is occupied either by self or someone else. It is God's plan for that same child as an adult to let God take control. For the allegiance to be centered on God. So, Jesus Christ becomes Lord of life. No longer does the self sit on the heart's throne, but Jesus Christ is the one in control.

When Jesus is Lord of our lives, we will put self-centered thoughts out of our minds. We will not allow ourselves to spend time thinking self-glorifying thoughts. Instead our minds will be focused on others, and how we can give ourselves to them. There is great joy in being free from self, and therein lies wonderful hope.

ﻪﻠﻪﻠﻪﻠ

Almighty God, thank you for setting me free from self. It gives me great hope to know you are in control of my life. Lord Jesus, take over my life completely. In your name. Amen

I want my ego to be dethroned from my life, so Christ can be my Lord.

Hope in Living in Reverent Fear

"If you invoke as Father the one who judges all people impartially according to their deeds, live in reverent fear..." I Peter 1:17

Peter wrote that we ought to live in reverent fear. This is to live in awe of God, which gives us hope. Awesome living before the Divine balances life. It humbles the soul, and allows God to guide one's living.

This is different than living in negative fear of God, which paralyzes us. It makes us ineffective because our minds race constantly in all directions disallowing concentration. Hurtful fear tenses our bodies and causes stress, which denies peaceful sleep and can even destroy us.

Many are afraid of entering relationships, because they require vulnerability. Others don't make career moves, because they are fearful of failure. Children and youth all over America are content with mediocrity, because of the fear of exploring new possibilities. Some do not smile, because they are afraid others won't smile back. We do not invest our energies in new efforts, because we don't have full assurance of success. Years ago I limited myself by clinging to an old electric typewriter, because I was afraid of not being able to learn how to operate a computer.

Peter wrote that there is a wholesome fear as well. We might call it a humble caution about life. It is living in amazement and wonder of God. Living in reverent fear allows us to humbly kneel before God opening our lives to receive divine grace. It means paying close attention to how we live. Most of all it means realizing that God is in charge, and God has laws that we are expected to live up to.

Paul wrote to the Christians in Galatia, "For freedom Christ has set us free. Stand firm, therefore, and do not submit again to a yoke of slavery." (Galatians 5:1) The apostle was writing that Christ set us free from the law, and one of the snares of that legalized living was fear. In setting us free from enslavement to law, Christ freed us from fearful living.

ﺎﻟﺎ ﺎﻟﺎ ﺎﻟﺎ

Merciful God, thank you so much for grace to live in awe of you. It gives us hope to know and to be amazed by your glory. Bless us with humility to live in reverent fear of you. In Jesus' name. Amen

I love the feeling of awe and amazement, when I consider the heavenly, mountainous clouds of God's glory.

Hope in Looking Beyond Our Problems

"Jesus said to her, 'Woman, why are you weeping? Supposing him to be the gardener, she said to him, 'Sir, if you have carried him away, tell me where you have laid him, and I will take him away." John 20:15

We can get so bogged down with our problems, that they keep us from seeing solutions. There is hope in looking beyond our problems.

It was Sunday morning, and still dark, when Mary Magdalene, one of Jesus' disciples, came to the tomb and found the stone rolled away. Frightened, she ran to tell Peter and another disciple. They ran all the way to the tomb, and found it empty as Mary said. Jesus' body was gone. The men returned home, but Mary lingered weeping outside the tomb. She looked inside, and saw 2 angels sitting dressed in white, where Jesus' body had lain. They asked, "Woman, why are you weeping?" She answered, "They have taken away my Lord, and I do not know where they have laid him." She then turned around, and Jesus was standing there, but her eyes were so filled with tears she did not recognize him. He said to her, "Woman, why are you weeping? Who are you looking for?"

Thinking he was the gardener, she said to him, "Sir, if you have carried him away, tell me where you have laid him, and I will take him away." Jesus then called her name, "Mary!" and she recognized him. Mary was so consumed by her worry, that her very response to her problem, namely crying, kept her from seeing her solution. Her tear filled eyes blurred her vision keeping her from seeing the answer to her question. She had come to the tomb to find the body of Jesus, but although he was directly before her she could not see him because of her tears.

All of us at one time or another have allowed our problems to blind us to solutions that stood right in front of us. Most often the solution is found in God, and we are looking elsewhere.

❧ ❧ ❧ ❧

All wise God, thank you for helping me look beyond my problems to the solutions found in you. Lift my eyes from the miry pit of difficulty to the glorious clouds of answers you have for me. In Jesus' name. Amen

Today, I will look beyond my problems to Jesus, who has solutions.

Day 43

Hope in Overcoming Worry

"So do not worry about tomorrow, for tomorrow will bring worries of its own. Today's trouble is enough for today." Matthew 6:34

Linguists tell us the word, worry, came from an Old English word, wyrgan, which meant, "to strangle." Dogs and wolves would go after the throats of their prey to strangle them. These beasts would wyrgan (worry) others. When we worry today, we strangle ourselves. Thus, worry is hurtful to us.

Jesus knew there was hope in overcoming worries, and so he said, "do not worry about tomorrow, for tomorrow will bring worries of its own." Destructive anxiety is from the devil, because it ties us into knots that keep us from our best accomplishments. We can get so involved in our problems, that our bodies are tense and our spirits taut. People high strung all the time are not their most effective selves.

God has a way to help us overcome worrying. Paul wrote about it to the Christians in the city of Philippi, "Rejoice in the Lord always; again I will say, Rejoice. Let your gentleness be known to everyone. The Lord is near. Do not worry about anything, but in everything by prayer and supplication with thanksgiving let your requests be made known to God. And the peace of God, which passes all understanding, will guard your hearts and your minds in Christ Jesus." (4:4ff) Putting our trust in God gives us great courage and confidence, because we know we are sustained by a power greater than us.

A wall plaque says, "Good morning. This is God. I will be handling all your problems today. I will not need your help. So, relax and have a great day." The relaxing part is good, but God does need our help. Paul wrote to the Corinthians, "For we are God's servants, working together." (I Corinthians 3:9a) We are co-workers with God. We need to trust God as though everything depends upon God, but we need also to work as though everything depends upon us.

One healthy way to diminish worry in our lives is to count our blessings. By being grateful for the many good things in our lives, we put out of mind nagging, anxious thoughts. There are indeed far more positives in our lives than we enumerate, and focusing on them eliminates worry.

ﭜﭜﭜ

Dear God, give me grace to trust in you, and not to worry. Help me to see that worrying hurts me, and help me be free of it. In Jesus' name. Amen

I will cast all my anxieties on Jesus Christ.

Hope in Wrestling with God

"Jacob was left alone; and a man wrestled with him until daybreak....
Then he said, 'Let me go, for the day is breaking.' But Jacob said, 'I will
not let you go, unless you bless me." Genesis 32:24 & 26

Jacob sent his servants with all of his possessions and his family across a ford at the River Jabbok. He was now alone at the river, and it was night. In the darkness a man approached Jacob, and they began wrestling. They wrestled all night, and when morning came, the stranger saw he could not win, so he struck Jacob's hip, and put it out of joint.

The stranger said to Jacob, "Let me go, for the day is breaking. But Jacob said, 'I will not let you go, unless you bless me.'" The stranger asked, "What is your name?" And he said, 'Jacob.' Then the man said, 'You shall no longer be called Jacob, but Israel, for you have striven with God and with humans, and have prevailed.' Then Jacob said, 'Please tell me your name.' But he said, 'Why is it that you ask my name?' And there he blessed him. So Jacob called the place Peniel, saying, 'For I have seen God face to face, and yet my life is preserved.'" Jacob found hope by wrestling with God until he was blessed. When dealing with God and life, we are blessed when persistent. God will give us a blessing, if we hang on and bang on the gates of heaven. Persistence with God takes grit, determination and courage.

In a parable Jesus told of a woman, who came to a judge begging for help, and initially he ignored her. However, she would not give up. Day after day she persistently came pleading, and finally because of her determination he granted her request. The single point of the parable is that through our faithful calling upon God, we too will be granted the things in life good for us.

A street man stopped in our church for food. After giving him some along with $5 we talked about work. He said he couldn't get a job. I said, "With all the 'help wanted' signs, why can't you find work?" I asked. "Do you ever cry?" I said, "Do not give up. Cry before God. Beg God for help." Knock on the doors of heaven until God blesses you.

Dear God, we wrestle with you not because you do not want to bless us, but we are so closed, that it is hard to be open to your blessing. Give me grace to bang on your doors today in order that I can receive your goodness. In Jesus' name. Amen

I want to be a more determined person to seek all the goodness God has for me.

Day 45

Hope in Being Alone

"But whenever you pray, go into your room and shut the door and pray to your Father who is in secret; and your Father who sees in secret will reward you."
Matthew 6:6

There is hope in being alone. Jesus told us in the Sermon on the Mount to go into the private rooms of our house to pray, It is so important for you to have time alone with God every day. It is only when you and I are alone with God, that God can deal with us and we with him.

Jesus practiced what he taught. He frequently went off by himself to the Mount of Olives for prayer to spend time alone with God. The night before he was crucified, he and his disciples were in the garden of Gethsemane. Taking Peter, James and John with him, Jesus told them to watch, while he went to be alone to pray. He was about to die, and in dealing with God he had to do that alone. When we are alone, only then can we deal with the depths of life.

There are three things that everyone has to do alone. One is to enter the world, and another is to leave it. We are born alone, and we die alone. But thirdly, we must deal with God alone.

If you have to be surrounded by people or noise to be comfortable, you are going to have to deny yourself that, if you want to deal most intimately with God. It is only, when you are alone in body and in mind, that God can reach us. People are a diversion, and noise can be a shield, where even God has a hard time getting through to you.

Our hearts yearn for this kind of intimate fellowship with God, because it fills a deep need in every one of us. On of the most enduring and popular hymns is titled, "In the Garden," and it begins with the words, "I come to the garden alone, while the dew is still on the roses, and the voice I hear falling on my ear, the Son of God discloses. And he walks with me, and he talks with me, and tells me I am his own; and the joy we share as we tarry there, none other has ever known" The intimacy of that private fellowship with God magnetizes every human heart.

Dear God, thank you for the intimacy I can have with you, when we are alone together. Help me to turn off the noise of the world and allow your Holy Spirit to commune intimately with me. In Jesus' name. Amen

I want to learn to love being alone with God.

Hope in Being Broken

"When the man saw that he did not prevail against Jacob, he struck him on the hip socket; and Jacob's hip was put out of joint as he wrestled with him."
Genesis 32:25

When we recognize our brokenness, then God can deal best with us. We become open to God, when we are humbled. Therefore, brokenness can bring us hope not available to us otherwise.

The conniving young Jacob decades ago, who stole his brother's birthright, was full of pride for his cleverness. Now in going back to face the brother he cheated, he had to return humbled. It is very humbling to lose part of your body, so the angel dislocated his hip. Now he would have to limp back to his brother, and therein was hope.

We have huge egos, and don't want others to see our weaknesses. God has blessed me with a good body. As a youth I played a lot of sports including being a member of a state tournament high school baseball team. I also played on my college tennis team briefly. At the age of 42 I developed a weakness in my left leg, which has left me with a limp. It was humbling, and we don't want to be humbled. God worked in my life through this limp in ways otherwise not available to God.

Acknowledging our brokenness is one of God's great gifts to us. Everyone has some weakness, some imperfection. Acknowledging our brokenness is used as a gift by God. Consider the times of growth in your life. Chances are they came after a failure or loss, when you were ready to receive new insights into life from God. A hurt man sat at my desk in tears, and I said to him, "This can become a wonderful opportunity for you."

We read in the book of Psalms, "The sacrifice acceptable to God is a broken spirit; a broken and contrite heart, O God, you will not despise." (51:17) Humbling ourselves before God provides God opportunity to do great things through us.

❦ ❦ ❦

Almighty God, thank you for the gift of being humbled. Forgive my pride and give me grace to kneel before you in body and spirit acknowledging you as my Lord. Thank you for hope through being broken. In Jesus' name. Amen

I want to be fully vulnerable before Jesus Christ today, and I want to see brokenness as God's opportunity.

Hope in Getting a New Identity

"Then the man said, 'You shall no longer be called Jacob, but Israel, for you have striven with God and with humans and have prevailed." Genesis 32:28

After Jacob had wrestled with the angel of God throughout the night at the River Jabbok, the angel wanted to be released. But, Jacob said, "I will not let you go, unless you bless me." The angel consented, and his blessing was a new identity with a new name. The angel said, "You shall no longer be called Jacob, but Israel, for you have striven with God and with humans and have prevailed." The name Israel means, "A prince of God."

Jacob had sullied his character and name as a young man by conniving and cheating. Through his faithful behavior since, he reshaped his life and received a new name. He was no longer a brother cheater, but rather now, "A prince of God."

Going through the early years of development causes us to do things we later regret. With the limited understanding, which naturally goes with having lived only 20 years, we do not know the ramifications of our behavior. Not having developed the self-control that goes along with growing years, we acted impulsively. God made us self-centered as babies, so we would survive. Without crying to get the attention of our parents, when we were hungry or hurting, they would not have known our needs and we would have died. However, many carry that infant need for self-centeredness into adulthood, and spend their lives crying for attention, when they ought to have grown to care for others.

You and I inherited names and then were given names as well. When we were young, like Jacob some of us did things that tarnished our names. Like Jacob we may have been selfish and dishonest, so our names were not looked upon with much respect. But like Jacob, God gives us another chance, and God helps us get a new name to win back respect.

By wrestling with God, we get a new name. A name of honor, Christian. As we put our faith in Jesus Christ, we too become members of the new Israel. Also being princes and princesses of God.

కు కు కు

Dear God, thank you giving me a new identity with dignity and honor. Help me to see myself today as a new person with new character, a child of God. In Jesus' name. Amen

I praise God for making me a new person with new identity.

Hope for Food That Satisfies

"Jesus continued, 'Do not work for the food that perishes, but for the food that endures for eternal life, which the Son of Man will give you.'" John 6:27

It was the day after Jesus had fed 5000 with five barley loaves and two fish, when some came to the place where the miracle had happened. Mark writes, "So when the crowd saw that neither Jesus nor his disciples were there, they themselves got into the boats and went to Capernaum looking for Jesus. When they found him on the other side of the sea, they said to him, 'Rabbi, when did you come here?'" Jesus did not respond to their small talk about travel arrangements. For him life was filled with larger issues, so Jesus answered them, "Very truly, I tell you, you are looking for me, not because you saw signs, but because you ate your fill of the loaves." The people had seen the great works of God providing a huge amount of food from 5 loaves and 2 fish. Jesus is telling the people they lost sight of God's work, and instead their minds were on their stomachs. "You didn't come looking for me, because your minds are fixed on God and his great work, but rather you are here, because you are hungry. You want more food."

Americans both overeat and under eat using food to control other uncontrollable factors in their lives. Some cannot have good relationships, but they can have good food. Others find life speeding out of control and unable to stop the world, but they know they can stop food and become anorexic. Someone has said, "We eat to forget, to remember to feel comforted, to feel stuffed, to be sociable, to be empowered." We can abuse food, but we all have to use it.

Most Americans eat too much, so our land is filled with overweight people. The apostle Paul saw the same misplaced values in his day. He wrote of such people to the Philippian Christians, "Their end is destruction; their god is the belly; and their glory is in their shame; their minds are set on earthly things." (Philippians 3:19)

We obviously have to take care of our physical needs by eating healthy and adequate foods, but Jesus said the physical alone would not suffice. By putting God first in our lives, we find the bread of life, which is Jesus Christ. Nurturing our spiritual needs with the food of God satisfies our lives, and we find strength to control our physical appetites as well.

Jesus said to a crowd, "For the bread of God is that which comes down from heaven and gives life to the world." They said to him, "Sir, give us this bread always."

Dear God, thank you for spiritual food that satisfies the deepest hungers of the soul. Help me to feed on Jesus Christ, the bread of life, who gives me strength to control the physical appetites of life. In his name. Amen

I want to feed mainly on God today, who will nourish my soul.

Hope in Refusing
to Repeat a Negative Past

"It has happened to them according to the true proverb, 'The dog turns back to its own vomit,' and, 'The sow is washed only to wallow in the mud.'"
2 Peter 2:22

Peter wrote these strong words in reference to people, who had become Christians, then reverted back to their previous ways of life. They had left previous licentious lives, when they knew no discipline. Those were days of living out of control. Then they came to know Jesus Christ, and felt the control of the Holy Spirit on their lives.

However, they turned back to their former lives, and Peter described it as a dog turning back to its own vomit, or a cleansed pig going back to wallow in the mud.

Many turn to Jesus Christ, who had not been entangled in messy lives of gross immorality. For them Christ has brought about new meaning internally, so their souls are renewed. Their hearts are filled with goodness. For them coming to Christ has brought about a whole new outlook on life.

However, others come to Christ being set free from self-abuse through alcoholism, indulgence in drugs, sexual promiscuity or angry living. Jesus Christ has made a dramatic difference in these people. Those around them observe the obvious and sometimes exciting change in their lives. Some come to Christ from secularism, or refocus their lives from TV and sports to serving Jesus through self-giving.

Peter wrote Christians giving up their faith to return to former ways were like "waterless springs" and "mists driven by a storm." (2:17) They were without the power of Jesus Christ, because they did not live closely to God. Spending daily time in prayer with God the Christian life is grounded, so we have strength to stay away from past negative behaviors. By living closely with Jesus Christ, we are filled with a sweetness that makes remembering our sordid past abhorrent. It is an ugliness we do not want to return to.

Dear God, thank you for setting me free from past sins, that were a drag on my spirit, and a blotch on my soul. I praise you for this wonderful liberation. Give me strength to stay close to you, and to never to return to that earlier vomit and mud. In Jesus' name. Amen

I love my new freedom in Jesus, and will not let myself be chained again by my negative past.

Hope in Being Sure of Our Faith

*"But I am not ashamed, for I know the one in whom I have put my trust
and I am sure that he is able to guard until that day what I have
entrusted to him." 2 Timothy 1:12*

In our politically correct society, there are some things you don't talk about, if you want to be accepted. We are very influenced by the whole concept of fitting in perfectly with everybody else's thinking. Someone said, "the fish is in the sea and the sea is in the fish." We are in society, and society is in us. Being politically correct is part of being American.

However, in wanting to fit totally into the fabric of society, we give up who we are, and therefore our faith is sometimes hidden. We tend to hide our convictions and beliefs, because we don't know how others would react to them.

James wrote about the hopelessness of doubting in prayer. He said being doubtful in prayer is "like a wave of the sea, driven and tossed by the wind; for the doubter, being double-minded and unstable in every way, must not expect to receive anything from the Lord."

Having strong faith bolsters our hope and gives us wonderful confidence to be open about it. Even though the apostle Paul was a convert to Christianity, he had overwhelming confidence in Jesus Christ. He wrote to his young colleague, Timothy, "...I am not ashamed, for I know the one in whom I have put my trust, and I am sure that he is able to guard until that day what I have entrusted to him." Paul was very open about his faith and confidence in Christ. There was no doubt in his mind that Christ was the son of God, and trusting him had value both for this life and the life to come. That gave him hope.

An important aspect of building strong faith is surrounding ourselves with people of strong faith. We grow with and through fellowship with others.

❧ ❧ ❧

Dear God, thank you for grace to have strong faith. I am grateful for the hope it gives me for this world and the next. Show me how I can strengthen my faith in Jesus Christ. In his name I pray. Amen.

I want rock like faith that will hold me up in all the storms of life.

Day 51

Hope in Not Being Imprisoned by Our Past

"But all shall die for their own sins; the teeth of everyone who eats sour grapes shall be set on edge." Jeremiah 31:30

God is saying in this scripture that children shall no longer suffer for their parents' failures. Most human beings feel linkage to the past, which they want to overcome. For some it was an alcoholic father or mother. Others came from a family without education, and they wanted to be the first to graduate from college. Children of divorced parents are often determined never to make their children suffer through a family break up. Youth from poverty backgrounds want desperately to excel the status of their parents.

Scientists have sequenced the human genome, which means the listing of all genetic material found in one cell. Two research organizations identified the 3 billion chemical letters that make up each cell. This now tells us how all human genes fit together. Medical people feel this will help us discover how to fight diseases.

However, some look upon our genetic structure as an imprisonment, whereby we are locked up to our past. The weaknesses of the parents will necessarily be our downfall as well. Their behavior will dominate their children's actions, and the children are not really free to break those historic bonds.

God gives us hope to break negative parental molds and freely choose our own course of life. Jesus Christ provides us with power to unlock family doors that have held us back. The free will God has given us is more powerful than our chromosomes.

Writing from prison, the apostle Paul pleads with his listeners in Ephesus, "I therefore, the prisoner in the Lord, beg you to lead a life worthy of the calling to which you have been called." He is saying you are bigger than your genes and your background. You have enormous power over your life despite any negative history. "I beg you to lead a life worthy of the calling to which you have been called." Your genes and your childhood environment are not holding you back. "I beg YOU to lead a life...." Paul is saying, "You have power over your life. Take hold of it and live in a manner worthy of your calling." By walking closely with God the Holy Spirit gives us power to live the will of God for us.

❧ ❧ ❧

Almighty God, I thank you for your power, which gives me strength to overcome my past. I praise you for this hope to be the person you want me to be. In Jesus' name. Amen

God will help me overcome negative family aspects of my past.

Day 52

Hope to Take Control of My Life

"We must no longer be children, tossed to and fro and blown about by every wind of doctrine, by people's trickery, by their craftiness in deceitful scheming." Ephesians 4:14

L iving by the values of the American society, we will be tossed about like a ship at sea. The movie, Perfect Storm, shows waves 100 feet high. Meteorologists confirm that ocean conditions can create waves that high, putting people near them in danger. Similarly, the destructive waving influences for immoral behavior are enormous, as historic values are being discarded. It is very sad seeing people even of high reputation caught up in internet immorality.

When we are not seeking the will of God, our lives are more easily tossed about by waves in life. The way to overcome these cultural forces is to live closely with Jesus Christ doing God's will. Because God is in ultimate control of life, it is utterly important to want to live at the center of his will.

It is a wonderful truth: the more God controls your life, the freer you become. The more control you give God the freer you will be. Living away from God and trying to live differently from his teaching, we are not strong enough to be in control of our lives. None of us is strong enough to contend with evil.

It is only when we acknowledge that God is in control, and we seek to live according to his will that we have power to conquer the problems of life. People in Alcoholics Anonymous and Gamblers Anonymous all speak the same language. In breaking free from addictions that controlled them, people say, "I had to learn that I am not in control of life, and have to humble myself under the hand of God, who is in control."

Paul writes we are responsible for our lives, but who has control of them? It is natural to think that if I am responsible then I have control. But that is not true. Paul tells us who is in control: "There is one body and one Spirit, just as you were called to the one hope of your calling, one Lord, one faith, one baptism, one God and Father of all, who is above all and through all and in all." (Ephesians 4:4-5) Even though we are responsible for our daily decisions and choices, nevertheless, God is ultimately in control of our lives. By living closely with God we are empowered to take control.

ᘓᓬ ᘓᓬ ᘓᓬ

Wonderful God, I am so thankful that you control my life, and by living with you, I have control. Help me to accept the discipline of your Spirit to live my life totally for you. In Jesus' name. Amen

Living a controlled and disciplined life is a great gift of God.

Hope in Living in Harmony with Others

"I therefore…beg you to lead a life worthy of the calling to which you have been called, …making every effort to maintain the unity of the Spirit in the bond of peace." Ephesians 4:1 & 3

God created us to live in harmony, and by opening ourselves to the daily influence of God, joyous accord fills our relationships. Naturally, it takes effort, but when we humble ourselves before Jesus Christ we more easily "maintain the unity of the Spirit in the bond of peace." Somehow sweetness enters the give and take of life. A positive spirit exists between us, and arguments seemingly disappear.

One of the best ways to make this happen is to pray for each other. By sincerely asking God to bless the important people in our lives, we will develop a wholesome feeling toward them. When anger develops in a marriage, praying for each other is one of the easiest ways to diffuse it. If each spouse will simply go to a quiet room, and pray repetitiously, 'Lord Jesus Christ, bless" than add the spouse's name, God will quietly instill in that prayer's heart a renewed love and sweetened feeling for that spouse.

In order to have happy relationships with those around us, we must have joy within us. If we are angry with ourselves, that anger will block happiness with those around us. The beginning of internal joy is to accept the glorious love God has for us in Jesus Christ. A heart that feels loved is much more likely to be a joyous heart, and a joyous heart will bring joy to those around it. John understood that, when he wrote, "Beloved, let us love one another because love is from God; everyone who loves is born of God and knows God." (I John 4:7).

The only way to unity is walking the path of humility. The path Jesus walked. Paul wrote to the Christians in Philippi, "Do nothing from selfish ambition or conceit, but in humility regard others as better than yourselves. Let the same mind be in you that was in Christ Jesus…" (Philippians 2:4-5) Having this humble mind brings hope for harmony in our lives.

ﻋﻠﻰ ﻋﻠﻰ ﻋﻠﻰ

Gracious God, help me to be a gracious person, one who is humble in heart. Enable me to build unity wherever I am. In Jesus' name. Amen.

I want to be a person who is used by God to bring harmony in life.

Hope Through the Wonder of Faith

*"Now faith is the assurance of things hoped for, the conviction
of things not seen." Hebrews 11:1*

A rummage sale was held by the Mother's Club of Seattle's Lakeside School in the spring of 1968. These caring parents spent many hours on this sale with the faith to buy a computer for the Lakeside students. The sale made about $3000, which would provide opportunity for their children to learn new technological skills. A seventh-grader, Bill Gates, played around on the computer, and through hard work made himself into a programmer. Before finishing high school he had started his own business, which today is the world's biggest software company. It all happened, because some mothers had faith that something good would come from their efforts.

The writer to the Hebrews defined faith with these words: "Now faith is the assurance of things hoped for, the conviction of things not seen." This is the only definition of faith in the Bible. We should commit this powerful verse to memory.

The word, assurance, in Greek literally means that which is put under, meaning that assurance is our foundation. Faith is the foundation of all the things we hope for. Whatever you want to happen is based on faith.

Faith is the conviction of things we do not see. Before something happens, faith is the certainty that it will take place. Faith is very important in all of life. Even when you are lying sick in a hospital bed. Though your body has been cut, or is not functioning as you wish, how it heals will depend to some degree on your faith. If you believe what has not yet happened, will indeed take place.

Believing God is going to create something good as you wait for a wedding, for a baby to be born, or for a company to call you after the second job interview. This is faith. It is the assurance of things hoped for, the conviction of things not seen.

Hitch your wagon to a star, and have faith that God is on your side. If you are seeking that which is in line with God's will, trust God wants to help you get it. Go after it with all your might. This will give you hope.

✤ ✤ ✤

Loving God, give me faith to believe you want the best for my life. Help me to go after my goals trusting you are working with me to achieve them. In Jesus' name. Amen

I believe that God will make real my dreams for life.

Hope in the Midst of Hardship

"By faith he (Abraham) stayed for a time in the land he had been promised, as in a foreign land, living in tents...." Hebrews 11:9

Abraham and Sarah left their home called by God to a new, promised land, which would be theirs. However, when they got there it was not an easy life, but rather one of great difficulty. By faith Abraham and Sarah persisted with hardship. Abraham and Sarah were full time campers in a foreign land living in tents. It wasn't just for a few nights, or during vacation. They could not escape to a Holiday Inn or Super Eight down the road. This was a way of life for them, and they did it by faith.

Many go camping in a tent for summer vacation knowing it is only for a few days or a week. If it is hot they say to themselves, "We can't wait to get home to air conditioning again." Or, if a thunderstorm passes by in the middle of the night with everything soaking wet, they are able to get into a dry car. Maybe even go to a motel.

Not Abraham and Sarah. This was a way of life for them, and they got through it by faith.

This experience implies hardship, and if you are experiencing difficulty in your life, the way to get through it is by faith. You may have problems with parenting right now. Or, your marriage isn't all you would like it to be. Perhaps, your work is stressing you out. Maybe your own health is giving you some concerns. Possibly you are having financial hardship.

God is able to help you get through it, as you trust in God's grace and mercy. We receive strength in weakness, and endurance in times of wanting to give up. Communing with God through prayer, we gain understanding on how to handle our problems. By reading God's word, we are assured of God's steadfast love in the midst of difficulties. Do not give up. God is on your side, so fill your heart with hope as God guides you through this negative period of life.

ello ello ello

Dear God, help me in the tough times. Strengthen me beyond my own strength. Give me understanding to know how to handle the difficulties. Bless me with patience and goodness. In Jesus' name.

Millions have walked the same path I am walking, and I know God will sustain me as God helped them.

Hope to Close the Goodness Gap

"For God so loved he world that he gave his only Son, so that everyone who believes in him may not perish but may have eternal life." John 3:16

A goodness gap has existed within every person since the fall of Adam and Eve. Their sin in the garden tainted all humanity with an inner struggle for righteousness. God intended to eliminate the evil of the world through Noah and the flood, but soon after the waters receded people went right back to evil. People ignored God. They lied, stole and killed each other. Brothers and sisters against brothers and sisters. Parents against their children, and children against their parents. Nation against nation. The rich sinned against the poor, and the poor stole from and killed the rich. Today the goodness gap is still one of the seven wonders of the world as big as the Grand Canyon.

You may be frustrated by thoughts you do not wish to have, or you have fresh regret for harsh words you spoke. You may struggle against emotional tugs to do things you do not wish to do. Or, you are irritated by not being disciplined to do the good you know you should be doing. Somehow you feel you do not measure up to what you think you ought to be and what God wants to you to be.

Take heart. When we put our trust in Jesus Christ, God gives us the righteousness that was in Jesus. Paul wrote we have the same gift God gave to Abraham. "Therefore his faith was reckoned to him as righteousness." (Rom. 4:22) Just by humbling yourself before Jesus Christ as your Lord, asking him to forgive your sins and walking with him, God considers you righteous. That means God gives you the righteousness that was in Jesus Christ. God closed your goodness gap. God accepts you as good and righteous as you put your complete trust in Jesus Christ and try to become like him.

And the beauty of your faith is that this is all a gift. Paul wrote again to the Christians in Rome, "For the wages of sin is death, but the free gift of God is eternal life in Christ Jesus our Lord." (6:23) We have a wonderful God, and a wonderful faith, so we receive goodness as a gift from God, because of what Jesus has done for us.

⚜ ⚜ ⚜

Dear God, thank you for giving me the gift of righteousness. Help me to accept it releasing the guilt that plagues me. Then give me grace to become like Jesus in all I do. In his name. Amen

I praise God for considering me righteous through my faith in Jesus Christ.

Hope for Living
from Resurrection Power

"I want to know Christ and the power of his resurrection...."
Philippians 3:10a

Paul wrote to the Christians in Philippi, "I want to know Christ, and the power of his resurrection." Hope for living victorious lives fills us now because of these words. Paul knew the power God used to raise Jesus was available to us, and he wanted that power to help him in his daily life. God's power of life is greater than the power of death, and God offers that strength to us. As God used his power to raise Christ with new life and a new body, God has power has to bring new life to us in this world. We have hope because God is constantly using his death destroying power to give new life to the hopeless. The Holy Spirit is able to resurrect hope in persons dead with despair, so they become alive and filled with excitement.

Can minds twisted with pornography be straightened? Can hearts captured by materialism be set free? Can spirits soured with anger, bitterness and resentment be sweetened with love and peace again? Can emotions deadened by adultery and alcoholism come alive once more? Can a ruined life be restored? Yes, by the power God used to raise Jesus from the dead.

It may take months or years to allow God to do this work of restoration, but lovingly and gently, divine healing takes place. Through the powerful mercy of God we can again become the people God wishes for us to be, and the people we so desperately wish to be. The creative resurrection power of God can renew us once more.

But it can only happen, if we are willing to die with Christ. Christ gave up his will and followed the will of God. As Christ gave up his will, we must give up ours. He did not want to die physically on the cross, and we do not want to die to self. Jesus' death cost him physical pain, and our dying to self hurts us, too. It hurts our pride. Bending our self-will is painful. Yielding control of our lives to God is not easy. Yet when we accept Christ into our hearts and die to self, God empowers us for new living.

Almighty God, thank you for power to live this life with victory. We praise you that you make available the power used to raise Jesus from the dead to raise us to new levels of life. In his name. Amen

God offers me resurrection power to lift my life to new horizons.

Hope to Experience Positive Change

"Do not be conformed to this world, but be transformed by the renewing of your minds, so that you may discern what is the will of God—what is good and acceptable and perfect." Romans 12:2

Change is the most constant thing in life. Everything is in continuing flux. Human behavior changes regularly, and Paul wrote to the Christians in Rome, that their change should be positive. There is hope in the midst of continuous adjustment.

Furthermore, he writes that we have a role in our transformation. Paul wrote, "Do not be conformed to this world, but be transformed...." This implies that we have power in this matter. Telling us to "Be transformed" implies we have a will that needs to be exerted. It means do what is in your power to be changed and different, and to close the goodness gap that exists in us. We have strength to determine who we will become.

However, it is not all up to us. God stands before us, beside us, behind us and within us to help us. God the Holy Spirit lives within us to encourage us and strengthen us.

How does God do this? How does God change us into being and doing that "which is good and acceptable and perfect?" Assuming we have completely turned our wills over to God, we have to live in close fellowship with God. That means to have an active prayer life. We need to talk with God not only daily but throughout the day. By praying we are transformed. I have a friend organist, who was an alcoholic in his younger years. He prayed to God, and overnight God took away his desire to drink.

We experience positive change, when our minds focus on Jesus with thanksgiving. So many good things happen to us daily, we constantly need to say thank you. One of the best ways to let God make you a wonderful person is if you can be a thankful person. Fill your days praising God for all the glorious gifts God gives you. We are changed into happier, contributory persons, when our hearts are full of gratitude.

But we also have to ask for guidance and open our hearts and minds to the Holy Spirit to direct us in our work, our actions and our relationships. Praying the Jesus Prayer, "Lord Jesus Christ, have mercy on me," is a way to open ourselves to God's mercy and goodness. God has wonderful mercy for all people, but it doesn't do us any good, if we aren't open to receiving it. An active prayer life gives us hope for positive change.

Dear God, thank you for hope to change in a wonderful and positive way. I praise you for the hope of becoming a very loving and wise person, who reflects godliness in every way. In Jesus' name. Amen

I am excited about positive change that can take place in my life.

Hope Through New Energy

Jesus said to them, "I am the bread of Life. Whoever comes to me will never be hungry, and whoever believes me will never be thirsty." John 6:35

Energy feeds life, and youthful energy brings excitement. In this text Jesus was not talking about physical food, but about spiritual nourishment. We have abundant hope, because we are resourced by eternal energy.

What strengthens you? What energizes you? Besides having shelter, basic to everything is sustaining our bodies. Sometimes our bodies are rested and we are well fed, so we have no hunger. Yet, something is missing. We are empty of certain energy.

I have been on vacation without any job responsibilities, getting good nights of rest while eating plenty of food. In the midst of that external restfulness I was empty of a certain energy, which could only be obtained by connecting with God through prayer. Just taking care of my body through food and relaxation was not enough. I needed God energy for my spirit.

Before he began his ministry, Jesus went out into the wilderness to be alone with God and to fast and pray. After being without food for a long time, the devil came to him saying, "If you are the Son of God, command this stone to become a loaf of bread." Jesus answered, "It is written, "One does not live by bread alone." Our Lord was saying, "Satan, you know I am physically hungry, but there is much more to life than having a full stomach." Jesus knew being nourished in spirit was equally as important as filling physical hunger.

Saint Augustine said, "Lord, our hearts are restless until they find their rest in thee."

There is a basic spiritual need in every human. It is a God-shaped vacuum only God can fill.

One of the beautiful stories in the Bible is about Jesus in the home of Mary, Martha and Lazarus. Jesus and Mary spent a lot of time talking. She was fed spiritually. Her life was filled and her spirit nourished just spending time with Jesus. Two thousand years later, we receive fulfillment in the same way. By spending it with Jesus Christ.

Dear God, thank you for nurturing us with the deepest energy found on earth. Through your Holy Spirit you give us a deep peace that strengthens us. Grant me this profound power to live a wonderful and strong life today. In Jesus' name. Amen

I will stay in close energizing contact with Jesus today.

Hope Through Family Harmony

"How very good and pleasant it is when kindred live together in unity!"
Psalm 133:1

A couple was getting divorced, and one of the children was having a tough time with it. The mother brought the child to talk with me, and as we sat in my office she said to her mom, "I know you and daddy think divorce is better for you, but it is not better for us kids." This innocent and loving child could have written the verse, "How very good and pleasant it is when kindred live together in unity."

The background for this scripture was the Hebrew custom of having relatives share grazing land, and that land was passed on from one generation to another. When someone's cattle or sheep began eating the grass from another's land, squabbles arose. Sharing land caused many arguments, disagreements and sometimes violence. The people back then understood, "How very good and pleasant it is, when kindred live together in unity!"

To have harmony among people there must be active and loving communication. This is true in families, businesses, communities, organizations and governments. Whenever people live in compatible relationships, there must be the sharing of information in conversation. It has to be active. Granted, active can mean different things to different people. Some people can be happy with few words spoken, while others enjoy jabbering all the time.

Not only must there be communication, but if there is to be harmony, the talk must be loving. Someone said, "Many can argue, but not many can converse." It is very easy for people to get into negative modes in life, when they only think critically of others. When negative thoughts constantly fill our heads, they usually spill out through our mouths. The brain and mouth aren't always connected, because we talk without thinking. But there is a negative nerve connecting the brain and mouth, so critical thinking usually gets said some way.

Paul wrote to the Christians in Ephesus, "But speaking the truth in love, we must grow up in every way into him who is the head, into Christ, from whom the whole body, joined and knit together by every ligament with which it is equipped, as each part is working properly, promotes the body's growth in building itself up in love." (Eph. 4:15)

❧ ❧ ❧

Loving God, thank you that you made us to live lovingly with each other. Harmonious living is so wonderful, as it brings peace to the soul and joy to the spirit. Help me to do all I can to bring harmony in all of my family. In Jesus' name. Amen

I love joyous relationships, and will do all in my power to create them today.

Day 61

Hope Through Compromise

*"Then Abraham said to Lot, 'Let there be no strife between you and me,
and between your herders and my herders; for we are kindred. Is not the whole
land before you? Separate yourself from me. If you take the left hand, then
I will go to the right; or if you take the right hand, then I will go to the left.'"*
Genesis 13:8-9

Harmonious relationships require the hope of compromise. Wherever humans coexist there are going to be differences. Differences of thought. Differences of opinion. Differences in language. And differences in how to do things. When living together as a family, these differences have to be acknowledged. Also, they have to be worked through, and that often necessitates compromise.

One of the most beautiful stories in the Bible is that of Abraham and his nephew, Lot. When God called Abraham and Sarah to leave their homeland to go to Canaan, Lot went with him. In their new land Lot had accumulated wealth owning many animals. The animals of Abraham and Lot were tended next to each other, and this caused strife. The herders taking care of their livestock got into many arguments, as the animals were encroaching on the other's grass.

Then we read these gracious words from Abraham in Genesis 13, "Then Abraham said to Lot, 'Let there be no strife between you and me, and between your herders and my herders; for we are kindred. Is not the whole land before you? Separate yourself from me. If you take the left hand, then I will go to the right; or if you take the right hand, then I will go to the left.'" Abraham, the older of the two, gave the younger Lot first choice of the land he would choose. Indeed, Lot looked about him and saw the plain of Jordan well watered with lush grass, and he chose what he felt was the best land. Abraham compromised for the good of the family.

In marriages there are usually many differences. One likes the house hot, the other cool. One wants the toilet paper coming over the top, the other from the bottom. One wants the closet doors open to air things out; the other wants the hallway neat with the doors shut. There are preferences of color for the house, and variations of thought about food and clothing. One likes romance in movies, while the other wants to watch sports. Resolving our differences requires compromise.

The humble spirit of Abraham facilitated the compromise with his younger nephew. There is hope for harmony in relational compromise.

∽∽∽

Loving God, thank you for the hope of compromise in the midst of conflict. Help me to be willing to settle differences with humility. Allow me the grace at times to give instead of demanding my own way. In Jesus' name. Amen

I want to be someone who resolves conflict with grace for harmony.

Hope Through Direction

"…Let us run with perseverance the race that is set before us." Hebrews 12:1b

The Christian life is an exciting journey with objectives. The writer to the Hebrews encourages us, "let us run with perseverance the race that is set before us." Faithful disciples of Jesus Christ have movement toward a goal. God does not call us to run around in circles, but gives a direction. We need a course to travel, a route with focus. A servant of Christ is not a drifter, aimlessly going about life.

The "race that is set before us" is to serve Jesus Christ with every ounce of energy we have for all the days of our lives. Christians are intentional about their daily living, doing those things that honor God and bring others to Jesus Christ.

God's people always have purpose. The children of Israel crossed the Red Sea into freedom only because they had liberty as a goal being led by Moses. After 40 years in the wilderness they had the goal of entering the promised land by capturing Jericho. "By faith the walls of Jericho fell after they had been encircled for seven days." (Hebrews 11:30) Jericho was a very strong, fortified city. Its huge walls seemed impenetrable. But the people of Israel had a goal of making that city theirs, and God told them to march around it in silence once a day led by seven priests marching in front of the ark. The priests were to carry trumpets made of ram's horn. On the seventh day they were to march around it seven times and then the priests were to blow their trumpets. All the people were to yell, "And the walls of the city will fall down flat." And they did. The only way you and I will knock down walls that keep us from victory is to have direction. We need to know what we are about, and keep that objective before us.

A good place to begin examining our goals is to ask questions, "What would Jesus have me do with my life this week?" "Am I using my time wisely for God? Do I try to make every minute count for my Master?" "Do I take enough time to connect with God in prayer?" "Is there room in my schedule to let's God's will ruminate through my spirit by reading God's word?" "What goals does God have for my daily work?" Or, "What goals do I have for letting God create more loving relationships in my life?"

ﻪﻠ ﻪﻠ ﻪﻠ

Eternal God, thank you for giving life meaning and order. I praise you for the gift of purpose and goals. Help me today and every day to give my life fully to you by listing tasks I believe you want me to accomplish. In Jesus' name. Amen

I want the excitement of living my life most effectively for Jesus Christ.

Hope Through Having Endurance

"To that end keep alert and always persevere in supplication for all the saints."
Ephesians 6:18b

The challenges of life are many, and the temptations to give up abound, but keeping on going gives us hope. To persist with determination requires special grace. Paul's call for the Ephesian Christians to "keep alert and always persevere in supplication for all the saints" is a call to be faithful in prayer. The emphasis on perseverance alludes to the previous verse in the text, "Pray in the Spirit at all times in every prayer and supplication."

Our greatest sustenance for keeping going is prayer. By humbling ourselves at the feet of God in prayer, God blesses us with Olympic grace. We are given strength beyond our understanding. Our spiritual muscles are enlarged enabling us to carry larger loads. Through daily and humble prayer, we realize that more noble goals for the glory of Jesus Christ are within our reach.

The Christian race is life long. We all get tired, when we don't feel like pushing on. Skipping worship is so much more attractive, than disciplining ourselves to do it. And we all hit dry, sandy deserts, where we just don't feel we are being nurtured. Nothing fills our emptiness, and our efforts at spirituality go unmet. But for those who persevere in the race, God says at the end, "Well done, thou good and faithful servant. Come and enter your eternal rest."

As we run the race of life with faith in Jesus Christ, God gives us endurance to pursue our goal. The writer to the Hebrews encourages us, "let us run with perseverance the race that is set before us." (12:1) This is a call to continue the long haul. It is easy to begin the Christian life, but hard to sustain it. Anybody can start going to church, but it takes persistence to continue. Starting a walk with Christ is simple, but it is difficult to continue.

Paul wrote to the Christians in Galatia, "You were running so well, who prevented you from obeying the truth?" (5:7) What has hindered you from continuing? Jesus told about people who heard the word of God, and they immediately followed with great enthusiasm. But like plants without roots, so as soon as the hot sun hit high noon, they withered and died.

But we have hope in walking with Christ, who gives us courage and energy to go on with victorious living.

Eternal God, you alone have the energy to keep me going. Help me this day to open my life to your Spirit, who will strengthen me to run the race of life with determination. When I feel weak, don't let me give up. In Jesus' name. Amen

I praise God for energy to walk with determination throughout this day.

Hope with Jesus as Our Model

"Let us also lay aside every weight and the sin that clings so closely, and let us run…the race that is set before us, looking to Jesus the pioneer and perfecter of our faith…" Hebrews 12:1b,2a

There is hope in making Jesus our model for life. As television is the greatest medium of communication in America it provides many voices calling us to follow them. Incredibly cynical, negative and sarcastic programs influence us to follow them. Sit coms and movies portray a sexual freedom very different from the wonderful, disciplined teaching of Jesus. People saturated with the licentious images of television find life empty, without order and purpose.

Christians move forward with Jesus as their model, who was the "pioneer and perfecter of our faith…" Americans of all ages are wearing bracelets and lapel pins with the letters, WWJD, "What would Jesus Do?" Others show the public those questions by wearing t-shirts or sweatshirts with those letters. That question, "What would Jesus do?" comes from a book by Charles M. Sheldon's book, *IN HIS STEPS*, written back in 1896. It has been revived with a flurry of influence 100 years later.

In following Jesus' personal model of holy, godly living we find true joy and freedom. Whereas permissive sexuality enslaves us, disciplined sex recognizes its beauty within marriage bringing liberty and fulfillment at its deepest level.

Paul encouraged us to make Jesus our model with the words, "Let the same mind be in you that was in Christ Jesus," then he tells of Christ's self emptying to be born in human form. Emptying ourselves of self is the most difficult human task. Pride and self-interest naturally dominate our thoughts and our actions. Putting thoughts of self out of our mind and focusing our minds on Jesus Christ and service for his kingdom is very difficult. However, herein lies guidance to the most wonderful life of true freedom and joy.

This is being truly born again away from the natural self-centeredness of infants to being oriented to care for others. It is being transformed from the kingdom of self to the kingdom of God. And herein is salvation in Jesus Christ by allowing him to be our model for life.

❧ ❧ ❧

Dear God, thank you so much for coming to us in Jesus Christ to give us a model both for living and for dying. I am grateful that following Jesus will give me true freedom and the deepest joy on earth. Help me to learn his word and to follow his example. In his name. Amen

I want to pattern my life after the life of Jesus Christ.

Hope in Facing the Fear of Death

"For I am convinced that neither death, nor life...will be able to
separate us from the love of God in Christ Jesus our Lord."
Romans 8:38a-39b

Common words on the lips of the risen Christ were "Peace be with you" and "Do not be afraid." He says those words to us today, as we face and fear death. Jesus undergirds the spirit with hope as we ponder life's end in death.

The body of each of us will die someday, but if we trust in Jesus, he says to us, "Do not be afraid." God has broken the power of death by raising Jesus, so do not be afraid. We do not want to die, but the eyes of all will someday close for the last time. And in that death we will be transformed to a higher life than we could have ever known here on earth.

That was the faith of Winston Churchill. He planned his own Anglican funeral service in St. Paul's Cathedral. The liturgy of the church was to be used including the great hymns of faith. He wanted a bugler to be positioned in one part of the dome, and at the end of the service he would play Taps, symbolizing that the end of the day of life had come for Winston Churchill. But at the other end of the dome, another bugler would then play the music of Reveille: "It's time to get up. It's time to get up. It's time to get up in the morning." Churchill believed that Taps would not be the last note for us, but rather Reveille. We do not need to be afraid, because as God raised Jesus, God will also raise us to a new day. The love of God will make the eternal arms of God feel even warmer in heaven than on earth.

As God loves us enough to give us a blessed life on earth, God will continue to love us in the next world. Paul wrote to the Roman Christians that "neither death, nor life...will be able to separate us from the love of God in Christ Jesus our Lord." Since God's love will be as strong in heaven, the Bible promises our life there will be even more glorious than the one on earth.

ﻌﻠﻌﻠﻌﻠ

Eternal God, thank you so much for hope in the face of death. Praise to you for giving us peace as we ponder eternity with you. May that peace replace our fear. In Jesus' name. Amen

Christ sets us free from the fear of death.

Hope in Being Filled with the Spirit

"Do not get drunk with wine, but be filled with the Spirit." Ephesians 5:18

The Ephesian Christians used to be pagans, who knew about the drinking parties of their day, called sumposiums. We have *symposiums*, where people get together for discussions, but the pagans 2000 years ago had *sumposiums*, where they were filled with liquor. These Christians remembered, when they tried to find happiness by filling themselves with wine, but now they knew that true joy comes from being filled with the Spirit of God. So, Paul writes, "Do not get drunk with wine, for that is debauchery; but be filled with the Spirit,"

A preacher once speaking on the subject of being filled with the Spirit opened his sermon with the words, "You've got to fill a person with something." Our minds and spirits are vacuums, that are going to have content, and the only question is, "What is in you? What occupies your mind, your heart and your spirit?"

We are changed when our minds are filled with the Spirit of God. When God the father of our Lord Jesus fills our minds, they have thoughts associated with Jesus. Instead of boredom there is excitement. Angry thoughts are replaced with those of joy. No longer pondering hate, the mind thinks about how to love and help people. Frustration is replaced with hope. Thoughts of lust centered on serving self now turn to thinking of serving others.

Hopeless people are limited by human vision. Filled with the Spirit of God, the mind now sees God possibilities. There are new vistas of opportunity.

Sometimes Christians live in the dog days of their faith. These are humdrum times, when there isn't much excitement. There may even be frustration, and it may be considered a down time. A desert period, where there is no lush grass of comfort and beauty. There is no oasis of joy with refreshing water. We have all lived in those spiritual dog days, and today's scripture gives us some insights on how to get out of them.

It is to be filled with the Spirit God. By centering all of our thoughts, words and actions on him, we are filled with God's Spirit. Reading the Bible with an open spirit to let the living Word of God saturate our very beings is to be filled with the Spirit of God.

Dear God, thank you so much for entering the core of my being, and saturating my heart, mind and soul. I rejoice at being filled with your Spirit. Fill me now and always. In Jesus' name. Amen

I want God's Spirit to fill all of me.

Day 67

Hope in Changing the World

*"But you will receive power when the Holy Spirit has come upon you;
and you will be my witnesses in Jerusalem, in all Judea and Samaria,
and to the ends of the earth." Acts 1:8*

There is hope to change the world, and some of that hope lies in you. Jesus spoke the words that God wants us to be witnesses to help change the world. As he came into the world to redeem it, Jesus wants to use us to do it. Instead of being changed by the world, Christians are to transform the world around them.

Jesus knew change in the world comes by changing people. Wherever we are, we can give witness to Jesus Christ. The fundamental witness we give is how we live. Instead of letting our lives take on the character of the world, which is evil, we are to present our lives completely to God through Jesus Christ, and thereby, God enables us to do what is "good, acceptable and perfect." The Christian can only be used to change the world for God, when we become like God.

Nearly two thousand years ago, a young Christian named, Telemachus, transformed his world with his witness for Christ. He was a farm boy in the Roman Empire, who as a young man decided to expand his horizons and see the attractions of the city. Coming into Rome he knew not where to go, so he followed a crowd, which led him into a coliseum. Seated among the throng he saw gladiators fighting to kill each other. With Christ in his heart, he knew this was wrong. So, he stood up and shouted, "Stop. Stop." People around him smiled thinking this was part of the show.

When those in the arena did not heed his call, he ran down the stone steps and jumped over the wall. Seeing the men flailing at each other with swords, he ran up to them yelling, "Stop. In the name of Christ. Stop. Don't hurt each other." Their huge arms with bulging biceps continued to thrust their swords. The crowd was having fun thinking Telemachus was a paid clown adding spice to the show. As the gladiators kept fighting he got between them, and a sword pierced his body, which fell to the ground, grew limp and died. Never again did gladiators enter the arena to kill each other. One young Christian transformed the world forever, because his life was literally a "living sacrifice, holy and acceptable to God."

❦ ❦ ❦

Lord of life, I want to be used to change your world today. Help me to be a godly example to all in my life today, and help me to say a word for Jesus. In his name. Amen

God needs me to renew the world, and I want to help.

Hope in Denying Ourselves

"For those who want to save their life will lose it, and those who lose their life for my sake will find it." Matthew 16:25

There is hope in laying down our lives for Jesus Christ, because in doing so we find life. By self-emptying we are filled, and by self-denial we are rewarded. The word, life, here refers not just to our bodies, but also to all we are. To our mental, emotional and spiritual selves.

In the eyes of the world, this is extreme living. Denying yourself and taking up another's burden, is contrary to the ways of the world. The world advertises self-indulgence. Get all you can. Feed yourself. Looking after anybody but number one is extreme behavior. But Jesus said that living as extremophiles by giving up own desires and following his purposes will give us true life.

Just as extremophilic microbes become useful living in environments that could kill people, Christians are to lay down their lives serving Christ even if it is hard for us. While serving others for Christ, even if it requires suffering, self-denial and loss of life, we gain new life we would not otherwise have had. Someone has written, "The divine irony of the gospel is that loss for Christ's sake leads to heavenly gain."

It has been written, "Sometimes life breaks us, but then we become stronger in the broken places. Sometimes challenges overwhelm us, but then we acquire wisdom that helps us to meet and overcome those challenges. Sometimes we lose our faith in people and in the world around us, but then our faith in God becomes more secure."

God has service opportunities for you today. Perhaps it is something special you can do for your family. If you are married, how can you serve your spouse better? Or, if you have children, how can you give yourself more to them as a loving parent? Do you have a friend with a special need that you could help fill? Or how about giving yourself to a neighbor in need?

What about your church? What are you doing for Christ to help your congregation? How are you laying down your life for your church? It is through losing yourself in the work of Jesus Christ, that you will find life in its fullest.

Dear God, thank you for giving me an example of self-giving in Jesus, who laid down his life, and then was exalted above every other name. Help me to lay down my life for others as he did for me. In his name. Amen

I want to spend the rest of my life giving myself for Jesus Christ.

Hope Through Worship

"Through him, then let us continually offer a sacrifice of praise to God, that is, the fruit of lips that confess his name." Hebrews 13:15

Christians around the world receive wonderful hope weekly as they humble themselves in worship of God. God does a renewing work in us, when we bow before God in worship, acknowledging the greatness of God.

The word, sacrifice, means something of value that we are willing to give. The writer to the Hebrews is saying we are to offer, to give, our praise as something important to God. That is what we call worship.

The word, worship, comes from the word, worth or worthy. It implies honor or dignity. And we think about worship principally as a prayer, a church service or a ritual.

Worship is a very broad concept, and being aware of what we worship is not readily apparent to us. But worship also involves extreme devotion and intense love or admiration. Being easily deceived, knowing what we love and admire is not always apparent. Our hearts and minds are very self-centered, and we rationalize life very effectively.

Examining our focus in life will help us determine what we worship. Ask how we spend the majority of our time. Americans spend 4-5 hours a day watching television, which tells us something about their deep devotion to that box. Where do we spend our money? On Sunday mornings instead of humbling themselves at worship, Americans worship at check out counters, as they are deeply devoted to shopping. Study your checkbook and your calendar, and you will get a good view of where your deep devotion in life is.

God does something beautiful to the human spirit as it is humbled before God adoring him as one's maker. The spirit is lifted to new heights of being, and the mind is focused on that which is good and essential. Quietness comes to the soul, which permeates one's being. We worship first to honor Jesus Christ, but in so doing there is reciprocity of grace, whereby we ourselves are enormously blessed.

Jesus made a habit of weekly worship, and as followers of Jesus we do the same. The writer to the Hebrews wrote, we should not neglect "to meet together, as is the habit of some." Millions have put it crudely, when they forsake worship saying, "The whole week is shot, I'm not going to church." God's fills us with hope through worship.

᪥ ᪥ ᪥

Dear God, thank you for humility to bow before you in worship. You are worthy of all my honor, and I praise you for the grace you give me through worship. Thank you for new strength and life that fill me through adoring you. In Jesus' name. Amen

I want to honor God with worship every week.

Hope in God's Faithfulness

*"God is faithful; by him you were called into the fellowship of his Son,
Jesus Christ our Lord." I Corinthians 1: 9*

Faithfulness builds hope, and all admire faithfulness. Paul's letter to the Christians at Corinth echoes faithfulness at its greatest, namely the faithfulness of God. Paul knew God had always been faithful to his people. He remembered the words of Moses, who had convened the people of Israel together for a large meeting. He told them they were a holy people chosen by God over all the people on the earth. Not because they were more numerous. In fact, they were the smallest nation. Moses said they were special, because the Lord loved them, and he brought them out of slavery from Egypt. God did that because he kept his promise to watch over them. Then Moses said, "Know therefore that the Lord your God is God, the faithful God who maintains covenant loyalty with those who love him and keep his commandments, to a thousand generations." Deuteronomy 7:9

Paul had experienced God's faithfulness, when he was shipwrecked, when he was chased out of town by angry mobs, when he escaped hostility climbing over city walls in the middle of the night, and when he was beaten. He also knew that God would be faithful to give him new life in the next life, so he wrote, "Death has been swallowed up in victory." "Where, O death, is your victory? Where, O death is your sting?"

When we are shown faithfulness, it is easier to imitate it. Having seen it, we are more able to do it. Our supreme model of faithfulness is Jesus Christ. The writer to the Hebrews wrote, "Therefore, brothers and sisters, holy partners in a heavenly calling, consider that Jesus, the apostle and high priest of our confession was faithful...." Hebrews 3:1-2a Jesus was sent into this world to redeem the world, and he was faithful even unto death.

God's faithfulness to love us and care for us enlivens our hope. We can put our final trust in God's goodness to us. Nothing in life gives us more assurance for living than leaning on God's kindness and strength.

☙ ☙ ☙

Ever-faithful God, I rejoice for the ability to stand on your promises to us. Thank you for the wonderful hope you give us. Having you as a solid foundation for life is so assuring. Keep my footing solidly on you today. In Jesus' name. Amen

I am amazed at God's wonderful faithfulness to me.

Hope in Overcoming Death

"Death has been swallowed up in victory. Where, O death is your victory?
Where, O death is your sting?" I Corinthians 15:54d-55

Nothing brings more fear in life than death. For the Christian, however, the sunshine of hope dispels the darkness of death. God destroyed the power of death by raising Jesus from the grave. There is no more need to fear. When Mary Magdalene and the other Mary got to the tomb on Sunday morning, there was an earthquake, and an angel rolled away the huge stone from the tomb. The angel said to the women, "Do not be afraid; I know that you are looking for Jesus who was crucified. He is not here; for he has been raised, as he said. Come, see the place where he lay."

The father of Robert Hughes mined coal in the northeastern hills of Pennsylvania. He had the dangerous job of checking the mine for methane gas before the miners could descend into the bowels of the earth. Every morning, carrying a safety light, he would go down alone into the mine. He checked every tunnel and shaft to make sure no deadly methane gas was present. If the light flickered on his safety lamp, he ran as fast as he could, because there might be an explosion. When he finished checking the mine, he climbed out to the surface above where miners were waiting for him. They waited for his announcement, "It's ok, it's safe, and you can now go down into the mine."

That is what Christ has done for us. He has gone down into the pit of death, and coming out he has announced to all of us, "It's ok. It's safe. You can enter death, into the darkness and the unknown. It's safe because I have been there and checked it out. I have overcome it."

Hope of eternal life in Christ sets us free to live more fully. Fear no longer stresses our bodies or harnesses our spirits. It is wonderfully liberating not to have the mind locked on our concern of death. We know we will move from this life immediately into one more glorious and wonderful when death overshadows us.

༄ ༄ ༄

Our death-destroying God, thank you for the hope of overcoming death with new life. This gives us freedom to live this life more fully, knowing there is nothing to fear. In Jesus' name. Amen

Through Jesus, death is an open door to a greater life.

Day 72

Hope in repentance

"In those days John the Baptist appeared in the wilderness of Judea
proclaiming, 'Repent, for the kingdom of God has come near.'"
Matthew 3:1-2

As God planned to come into the world in Jesus Christ, God sent a man named John the Baptist to prepare the way. John was bold and unusual. He wore rough clothing made of camel's hair with a belt around his waist. Grasshoppers and honey were his diet. He was his own man, who marched to the beat of a different drummer.

Not only was he rough, but he also separated himself from people. Matthew writes, "In those days John the Baptist appeared in the wilderness of Judea." But he had magnetism, so "the people of Jerusalem and all Judea were going out to him." (3:5) Rumor spread in cities about this fascinating man out in the country, who miraculously drew a crowd, where crowds seldom gathered.

What did they hear? Shockingly they went out into the wilderness to hear these words, "Repent, for the kingdom of heaven has come near." As he prepared the way for the coming of God, John called people to repentance.

What does the word mean? We often associate repentance with an intense emotional experience. It does involve remorse, a feeling of sorrow for a misdeed. However, if repentance stops at venting sorrowful emotions, then it is empty. The final conclusion of repentance is change of behavior. When John the Baptist called people to repent, he had in mind a change of life. True repentance means turning from wrong doing to a life of righteousness. Repentance means change.

When we truly repent, it must be evidenced in our lives. John the Baptist said, "Bear fruit worthy of repentance." If you have really turned from doing wrong, it will be seen in your daily life.

How do we receive strength for bearing fruit? John the Baptist said he came calling people to repentance, but Jesus would come to empower them. John said Jesus "will baptize you with the Holy Spirit and fire." Through faith in Jesus Christ we receive the Spirit of God in our lives to enable change of behavior. It is the kind of strength that Paul meant, when he wrote in Philippians 4:12, "I can do all things through him who strengthens me."

❧❧❧❧

Almighty God, thank you so much for helping me change my life. It is so wonderful to have the strength to turn from self-centered living to living for you. My life feels so clean in this wonderful process. In Jesus' name. Amen

I want to keep repenting until my life is fully congruent with God's pattern for me.

Hope in Righteous Living

"Both of them were righteous before God, living blamelessly according to all the commandments and regulations of the Lord." Luke 1:6

Living faithful, moral lives before God mysteriously brings hope. Hope has eyes that look to the future, and living righteously tends to make us look ahead eliminating backward looking guilt.

The priest, Zechariah, and his wife, Elizabeth, were "righteous before God, living blamelessly according to all the commandments and regulations of the Lord." These honorable parents were given a son, who would be known as John the Baptist, whom Jesus called the greatest of prophets.

It takes the strong morality of parents like Zechariah and Elizabeth for God to create a strong child like John the Baptist. Children need to see this kind of modeling for them to have inner strength to walk up rightly against the winds of life. Their son, John, gained faith from them enabling him also to have a close relationship with God.

God created us with moral integrity, and living with that integrity brings much peace. Living out the image of God within us, strengthens the spirit, clears the mind, deepens the soul and even enhanced physical well being.

God created us to enjoy us and God, as our heavenly parent, wants to bless us with moral strength to make sure we are healthy and safe. As human parents want their children happy, God wants us to have joy. Jesus said, "I have said these things to you so that my joy may be in you, and that your joy may be complete." (15:11) God came to us in Jesus, because God wants to give us all the goodness life can afford. That can best happen by walking on the moral high road of life.

Just before God gave the ten commandments to Moses, God said, "I am the Lord your God, who brought you out of the land of Egypt, out of the house of slavery..." Those words are a promise to us. Before God gave us commandments to live by, God promised always to be our God. As God is faithful to us, God gives us grace to keep the mind focused on loving God, and to center our spirits on loving others. Therein lies righteousness, which gives hope.

☙ ☙ ☙

Dear God, thank you for guiding us to live with moral integrity and strength. The wholesome feeling from this focused living encourages hope within me. Help me today to delight in your ways, and to center my whole being on serving you. In Jesus' name. Amen

I want to walk in the righteousness of God, as Zechariah and Elizabeth did.

Hope in Being Remembered by God

"I will remember in their favor the covenant with their ancestors whom I brought out of the land of Egypt." (Lev. 26:45)

We have a remembering God. God's children had been slaves in Egypt for many years, and they were harshly treated. But God remembered them, and delivered them. A miracle was performed, when half a million people crossed the Red Sea into freedom. Because it was such a historic experience, God told the Israelites to remember that occasion.

Even when we fail God and feel very guilty about what we have done, if we humble ourselves and ask for pardon, God will remember us and forgive us. God said, "I will remember in their favor the covenant with their ancestors whom I brought out of the land of Egypt." (Lev. 26:45)

God remembers nations as God told the Israelites, "if my people who are called by my name humble themselves, pray, seek my face, and turn from their wicked ways, then I will hear from heaven, and will forgive their sin and heal their land." (7:14) God will remember us, when we turn to him.

When you are down about anything, God remembers you. Your heavenly Father will not forget you. Jesus said, "Lo, I am with you always." No matter what you are wrestling with, God remembers you. You are not only on his mind, but the Holy Spirit is doing battle for you. The Holy Spirit is praying for you.

When children bring disappointment to a parent, the wise parent does not continue to remember that misbehavior. That is where the Psalmist was, when he wrote, "Do not remember the sins of my youth or my transgressions..." Don't recall all the bad stuff about us, O Lord. Please don't focus on that. What should God remember then? When we fail God daily by ignoring him, what is God to remember about us? The Psalmist suggests, "...according to your steadfast love remember me, for your goodness' sake, O Lord." (Ps. 25:7b)

God listened to the Palmist and remembered him not for the Psalmist's sins, but rather from the goodness of God's heart. God remembered all humanity in the most beautiful way by coming to earth in human form to take the sins of people upon himself in Jesus Christ. God's love remembered and is remembering us. The Psalmist wanted to be remembered, and God did.

ৎৣ৵ ৎৣ৵ ৎৣ৵

Dear God, thank you for not forgetting me. My heart is warmed to know that I am always on your mind, and that in your heart you want the best for me, your child. Help me to live in that comforting thought today. In Jesus' name. Amen

I am so thankful to be remembered by God.

Day 75

Hope in Remembering God's Grace

"Remember this day, in which you came out of Egypt, out of the house of slavery, because the Lord brought you out from there by strength of hand..."
(Ex.13:3)

It is healthy and hope building for us to be a remembering people. After God delivered the Israelites out of Egypt, Moses said, "Remember this day, in which you came out of Egypt, out of the house of slavery, because the Lord brought you out from there by strength of hand..." (Ex.13:3) Jews and Christians alike remember this event that took place over 3000 years ago.

Remembering God's goodness to us in the past gives us hope for the future. Special past graces are time markers that anchor God's wonderful kindness in our hearts and minds. When we were healed of an illness or a broken relationship was gloriously restored, we know God has been active in our past. When God gave us a better job, as the old one sadly ended, God's grace was evidenced. If God was merciful in the past, God will be merciful again in the future.

We need to remember what God has done for us. As Christians we celebrate by remembering God's past works for us. It was supremely manifested in God's coming to us in Jesus Christ, the Word of God made flesh, who dwelt among us. Jesus gave up a life with God and humbled himself to live among people. There is no human comparison. We can think of a queen giving up her castle to live in a tent, but that is not adequate. We can think of a human being willing to become an ant, but that is too small an exchange. We can only humble ourselves and accept the magnificent gift of Christ's incarnation. His coming to us in the flesh.

As we remember Jesus coming to us it was for our sin. And it is healthy for us to remember our need, confess it, accept God's forgiveness and then move on. God came to the earth with a mission, and that was to ultimately take our sin upon himself.

It is healing to recall our past sins, and lift them up to God. Then we can live in glorious freedom.

꧁꧂

Dear God, thank you for your wonderful work in my life. Keep ever in the front of my mind and in the center of my heart your great kindnesses to me. May they be strong reminders of what you are able to do again and again daily in my life. In Jesus' name. Amen

I am exicted that Jesus is able to repeat in my life wonderful experiences of the past.

Day 76

Hope in Being Saved

"(God) has raised up a mighty savior for us in the house of his servant David..." Luke 1: 69a

Zechariah talked about the birth of Jesus with those words. The "mighty savior" referred to Jesus, whose name comes from the Hebrew name, Joshua. The name Joshua means, "God is salvation."

There is hope in being saved from our self-centeredness, which often hurts us. By focusing just on ourselves we get into lots of trouble. We make mistakes, and then lie to cover them up. We are lazy with our minds, and do not think clearly as we ought. Centered on our own agenda, we ignore the will of God behaving foolishly and hurting others. Although God has given us power over our minds, we allow angry, hateful and negative thoughts to control them.

Jesus Christ, our savior, came to save us from ourselves and from sin. The beauty of the Christian faith is that being saved is a gift. God does the saving, and we only have to allow ourselves to be saved. Paul wrote to the Christians in Ephesus, "For by grace you have been saved through faith, and this is not your own doing; it is the gift of God-not the results of works, so that no one may boast." (2:8)

In September, 1860, the Lady Elgin was carrying 400 passengers on lake Michigan from Milwaukee to Chicago to hear Stephen Douglas. On the return trip it collided with the schooner, Augusta, off the shores of Evanston, Illinois. The ship began to sink, and cries for help sounded. A student from then Garrett Biblical Institute on the shore heard the cries for help. The water was rough, but Edward Spencer was willing to dive into the cold water to try to save passengers. He swam out to the boat, and brought in a passenger. His body and spirit struggled as he fought the high waves. How many times would he dive into that water? Two, three, four or five? After saving the seventeenth person, he nearly collapsed on that September beach. Afterwards he was so weak he had to be wrapped in blankets and given stimulants to restore him. While fading into unconsciousness, he asked, "Did I do my best?" Edward Spencer never recovered from that courageous act of sacrifice. He had to drop out of school, and although he lived to 81, he was never well again. His brother said he put into that one day "the struggle of three score years and ten." Like Edward Spencer, Jesus Christ came to bring us in from the cold, dangerous, and stormy, waters to put us on dry land and restore life. There is hope in being saved.

༄ ༄ ༄

Dear God, thank you for saving me to yourself and thus giving me new life. In Jesus' name. Amen

I want desperately to be saved from sin and from selfishness.

Hope in Being Blessed

"My soul magnifies the Lord, and my spirit rejoices in God my Savior, for he has looked with favor on the lowliness of his servant." Luke 1:46-48a

Mary, the mother of Jesus, spoke these words after she learned of her pregnancy. Through an angel Mary discovered God had chosen her to bring God's son into the world. After Mary became pregnant through the Holy Spirit she went out into the hill country of Judea to see her relative, Elizabeth. According to Luke's gospel, when Elizabeth met Mary she said, "Blessed are you among women, and blessed is the fruit of your womb." Mary had faith in a gracious and merciful God before whom she knew she was special. She knew God was on her side, and on the side of those who trusted in God. This was her identity.

You are a blessed person created and loved by God, and having that identity of being blessed makes a tremendous difference in how you get along in life. The identity you have will determine how motivated you are. If you see yourself as isolated, feeling the world is against you, it drains your strength. You begin asking, "What is the use?" Those who think the world is always throwing stumbling blocks will soon give up, and live without hope.

Although for different reasons, God says to you what God said to Mary, "Blessed are you. I made you and put you into this world, I will do everything I can to help you. It is important for you to know that I, God, am on your side." God is bigger than the world and in charge of the world. God is on your side. God loves you, and wants desperately for you to have a wonderful life. God is your cheerleader.

As Paul asked the Christians in Rome, "If God is for us, who is against us?" (Romans 8:31b)

Rhetorically he was saying with God as our supporter nothing else matters. If you are blessed by God, you have hope in all situations. No matter what your plight, what your struggles, if you are honoring God with your life, and trying to live for Jesus Christ the best you can, God is on our side. God wants you to succeed.

❧ ❧ ❧

Dear God, thank you that I am special in your eyes. Help me this day to see that I am blessed by you, and give me eyes to see the sun shining on everything I do today. In Jesus' name. Amen

I rejoice because God is for me, and the world is not against me.

Hope in a Personal Relationship with God

"See what love the Father has given us, that we should be called children of God; and that is what we are." I John 3:1

There is nothing more glorious on earth than having a personal relationship with God through faith in Jesus Christ. This intimate connection with God elevates the human spirit to another level of life. Human relationships are wonderful and utterly necessary, but no human association brings the depth of fulfillment that connecting with God does.

Today as in the day of John the Baptist people are often content having a relationship with God only by association. The Israelites long ago said they were ok with God because they were blood relatives of Abraham and Sarah, founders of the Jewish faith. But this was one instance in life, when connections didn't matter. John the Baptist said to them, "Do not begin to say to yourselves, 'We have Abraham as our ancestor'; for I tell you, God is able from these stones to raise up children to Abraham." He was saying that a personal connection with God was important.

What was at issue here? The people were making excuses for how they were living by saying; they were favored by God because of their ancestral heritage with Abraham. "I have the blood of the father and mother of our faith, Abraham and Sarah, running through my veins. Therefore, I am part of the in-crowd. I am part of God's select few because I was born into it." John the Baptist says, "No, you can't be born into it. It doesn't make any difference what your name is, what your family tree shows, what your pedigree boasts." If you are a child of God it is because of your own behavior and nothing else.

Becoming a parent is an amazing experience, and is surpassed only by becoming a grandparent. It makes an old man and old woman become giddy and childlike again. But this is one way we differ from God. Only people have grandchildren. God only has children, because every human being must become a child of God through a personal relationship with Jesus Christ. This relationship can't be inherited. If you are a Christian it is because you personally have invited Jesus into you heart.

☙ ☙ ☙

Dear God, thank you for this amazing gift of being able to relate directly with you, as if I were the only person on earth. This is a very humbling gift, and I rejoice in it. Give me grace to keep this relationship with you alive throughout my life. In Jesus' name. Amen

I praise God for the amazing gift of being a child of God.

Hope in Living Without Fear

"Surely God is my salvation; I will trust, and will not be afraid, for the Lord God is my strength and my might; he has become my salvation." Isaiah 12:2

Feelings of fear strike all, and not all fear is bad. Often fear protects us from wrong and hurt. However, fear is also debilitating. It can cripple the spirit, distract the mind and cause injurious stress to the body. As parents want their children free from hurtful fear, so God wants you, God's child, free from anxious feelings that hurt you and diminish your effective daily living.

The people of Israel were enslaved in Babylon. They lived in fear of being mistreated, and were afraid they would never be allowed to return to their beloved homeland on the Mediterranean Sea. Isaiah told them God is faithful and would deliver them to freedom at home again. The prophet said to them, "You will say in that day…Surely God is my salvation; I will trust, and will not be afraid, for the Lord God is my strength and my might; he has become my salvation." These are words of deliverance God gave the people of Israel.

Christians are singing people, and singing dispels fear. The apostle Paul and Silas were imprisoned for their faith, and at midnight they sang hymns. Singing turns our minds from fear.

When God came to us in Jesus Christ, God shared a message diminishing fear. The angel, Gabriel, came to Mary, and said, "Greetings, favored one! The Lord is with you." It was understandably very confusing to Mary to learn she would have a baby. The word, angel, means messenger, and Gabriel, the messenger of God, said, "Do not be afraid, Mary for you have found favor with God." Shepherds were in the fields watching their sheep that night. Suddenly a heavenly spotlight brightened the sky, and an angel stood before them. Luke wrote that the shepherds were terrified, and the first thing the angel said to them was, "Do not be afraid…" God wanted to dispel their fear.

God wants to dispel your fear. Paul wrote to the Ephesian Christians, God "chose us in Christ before the foundation of the world to be holy and blameless before him in love." You are also special to God. Even before God created and organized the galaxies, God had a dream of you as a special person to love. As you wrestle with fear, believe God is on your side. You are chosen and precious to God.

এএএ

Dear God, thank you that you want my life lived without fear. I am so glad you want my mind, soul, and spirit free from stressful anxiety. Take away my hurtful anxieties now. In Jesus' name. Amen

I will trust God today, so I will not be afraid.

Hope in Being a Slave to Christ

"Paul, a servant of Jesus Christ, called to be an apostle, set apart for the gospel of God..." Romans 1:1

Paul begins his letter to the Christians in Rome, "Paul, a servant of Jesus Christ, called to be an apostle, set apart for the gospel of God..." This is the only book Paul wrote, where he had never met his readers. They knew him only by name, so he wanted to identify with them. Many of the Christians in the church in Rome were educated slaves of high-class people. From recent American history, mention the word, slave, and a black face comes to mind. But in the Roman Empire, which had a huge percentage of slaves, they were mostly white.

The Greek word for slave is *doulous*. Translators use the English word, servant, but the Greek word, *doulous*, meant slave. Paul identifies with the Roman Christians by saying he too is a slave, but a slave of Jesus Christ. A slave is someone, who lives under the direction of some person or something.

There is great hope in being a slave of Jesus Christ. Martin Luther said, we are most free, when we are most enslaved to Christ. Although Paul was a slave of Jesus Christ, he found his true freedom in Christ. As he wrote to the Galatian Christians, "For freedom Christ has set us free; do not submit again to the yoke of slavery." (5:1)

Paul wrote his letter to the Roman Christians saying he was a slave of Jesus Christ. In fact everyone is a slave of something or someone. The only question is: to what or to whom are we enslaved? Americans are often enslaved with a focus on material things. A huge temptation for everyone is to become a slave to self, which will lead us to selfish behavior hurtful to our relationships and often even to ourselves. Becoming enslaved to Jesus Christ frees us from bondage to self. It can be important even to our mental health and our peace of heart. Being chained to Jesus Christ gives us the greatest hope in this life.

Lord Jesus Christ, I want to be a slave to you, so that I can be truly free. Help me to walk very closely with you, so my whole life is caught up in you and your work. In Jesus' name. Amen

Am I enslaved to Christ or something else?

Hope in God's Encouragement

Jeremiah said, "'Ah, Lord God! Truly I do not know how to speak, for I am only a boy." But the Lord said to Jeremiah, "Do not say, 'I am only a boy';...for I am with you to deliver you." Jeremiah 1:67a,8b

Fear and doubt assail all. Questions about our abilities and effectiveness plague everyone. Are we doing the work we ought to be doing? How can we be more effective? How can we guide our children more thoughtfully? What can be done to repair a broken relationship?

We all need affirmation and encouragement to live life more wonderfully, and God is the great encourager giving us hope.

Jeremiah was a man of faith, who was called by God to exercise that faith by being a prophet. Jeremiah's father, Hilkiah, served as a priest in the city of Anathoth. As his father was a clergy, no doubt Jeremiah got religious training in the temple, and began thinking about following in his father's footsteps. He might have thought he would become a priest, and take a little synagogue in the country, where it was quiet and he could live an easy life.

But God had other plans. Jeremiah himself wrote how the word of the Lord came to him saying, "Before I formed you in the womb I knew you, and before you were born I consecrated you; I appointed you a prophet to the nations." Being a prophet is not what Jeremiah had in mind. He had been thinking about being a priest, which is a quiet, non-controversial job. Go to the temple, say some prayers with the people and perhaps offer a few sacrifices. A prophet was confrontational. People got mad at prophets, and kings sometimes chopped off their heads. Being a priest would allow Jeremiah to spend his time in the quiet country villa. Becoming a prophet would no doubt require him to go to the loud and dangerous city

Jeremiah was afraid of this prophetic call, and claimed he was incapable of fulfilling it. Being a prophet would require speaking skills he did not have plus he thought a prophet must have a certain maturity he had not attained. So, he told God, "Truly I do not know how to speak, for I am only a boy." God encouraged Jeremiah with the words, "Do not say, 'I am only a boy'; ...for I am with you to deliver you."

As God calls you today to give yourself in various places, God stands beside you speaking the words he said to Jeremiah, "I am with you to deliver you." No matter what struggles you have today, God is with you to deliver you.

❧ ❧ ❧

Dear God, thank you that you are the great deliverer. As I get caught in difficult binds of life, I am grateful you are there to free me and lift me to new levels. Help me to feel you doing that for me right now. In Jesus' name. Amen

The Holy Spirit, the great comforter, is with me to strengthen and encourage me.

Hope in Overcoming Excuses

*Gideon said, "But sir, how can I deliver Israel? My clan is the weakest
in Manasseh, and I am the least in my family." Judges 6:15*

Go d needs people to do wonderful ministry in God's work at redeeming the
world. That includes God's needing loving parents to care for their children.
God needs the rich to look after the poor. The strong to care for the weak. The
faithful to love and help the misdirected. The clear headed to relate to the
confused. We are called to give ourselves to God's glorious redemptive work
today.

However, we have our excuses for not getting involved, but we are not unique
as the Bible is full of "only excuses." Moses told God he could not measure up to
Pharaoh, because he was only a shepherd. He also said he couldn't talk. When
God called Gideon to deliver Israel from Midian, Gideon told God, "I am the least
in my family." When David offered to challenge Goliath, Saul said to him, "You
are just a boy." Solomon was offered the kingship like his father David, but he
said, "I am only a little child." When Jesus asked his disciples for something to
feed 5000 people, they said, "We have nothing here but five loaves and two fish."

The Lord told Jeremiah he wanted him to be a prophet. But Jeremiah was not
expecting this, nor did he want to do it. He began feeling uncomfortable. Sweat
forming on his brow was not from the middle-Eastern sun but about this divine
appointment he didn't like. He wanted to obey God as his father did, but he
twisted and turned trying to get out of this one. Jeremiah had to rationalize his
excuse, so he said, "Ah, Lord God! Truly I do not know how to speak, for I am only
a boy."

We tell God, "I am only." In fact, God calls people not looking for the most
qualified, the most charismatic, or the most capable. Certainly, God needs people
with bright minds, with much organizational skill, and with leadership abilities.
And, God uses many such persons today toward great accomplishments. Most of
us fall in the "I am only" category, but God can do great works through "I am
only" people.

God is most able to use people, who are available to God. People who are
committed.

ﻪﻠﻟﺍ ﻪﻠﻟﺍ ﻪﻠﻟﺍ

*Dear God, thank you that you have a ministry for me, where I can be used for
the building of your kingdom. I want very much to be involved in the excitement of
bringing new life to others for Jesus' sake. In his name. Amen*

**I know self-giving for God gives me hope, and God will provide the grace
to do my ministries.**

Hope in Avoiding Hurtful Associations

"When you come into the land that the Lord your God is giving you,
you must not learn to imitate the abhorrent practices of those nations."
Deuteronomy 18:9

All people are composites of the persons in their lives. Therefore, people at every age need to be aware of their associations, as the people around us influence us. This is particularly true of young people, who are early in the process of character formation. However, even senior citizens, who have had thousands of contacts over their years, are still susceptible to change caused by acquaintances and friends. Because negative associations make us negative, they are to be avoided, and God gives us strength to do that.

The people of Israel had been led out of slavery from the land of Egypt. They were wandering in the wilderness, and God was bringing them to the land he promised them. As they neared that time, Moses told the people "When you come into the land that the Lord your God is giving you, you must not learn to imitate the abhorrent practices of those nations." The people living in the land God was going to give his people practiced ungodly behaviors. For example, there was an ancient practice of building fires, through which they made their sons and daughters pass. This was supposedly done to show the devotion the people had to their god, named Molech. Apparently, if their children died or their bodies were deeply wounded, it was considered a loving sacrifice to Molech. They also practiced magic, fortune telling and talking with the dead through séances. Moses exhorted the people not to be influenced by these people.

People around the whole world struggle with this teaching of Moses. Just as the Israelites would be tempted to be like the people in the lands they were entering, we are tempted to be like the people living around us. We tend to become like the people we spend time with. Their language becomes our language. Their way of thinking infiltrates our minds. We begin to imitate their mannerisms. Their way of doing things. Spending time with others changes our attitudes to become like theirs. Every reflective person knows social pressure influences us.

To help the Christians contend with outside influences in his day, Paul wrote, "Do not be conformed to this world, but be transformed by the renewing of your minds, so that you may discern what is the will of God—what is good and acceptable and perfect." Romans 12:2

Dear God, thank you for wisdom to choose good, positive friends, who will be a blessing to me. I am grateful for strength to dismiss behaviors seen in others that would be hurtful. In Jesus' name. Amen

To honor God, I will choose my friends and associations wisely.

Hope in Being Graced by God Through the Bible

"All scripture is inspired by God and is useful for teaching, for reproof, for correction, and for training in righteousness, so that everyone who belongs to God may be proficient, equipped for every good work." II Timothy 3:16-17

Without an objective guide to living, we would be condemned to a subjectivity that would lead to death. The Bible is that wonderful objective guide, wherein God blesses us with help to live victoriously.

Because God inspired the scriptures, they in turn inspire the hearts of people. For example, the Book of Psalms is a fountain of grace, where we read, "Gracious is the Lord, and righteous; our God is merciful." (116:5) Or, "O give thanks to the Lord, for he is good; his steadfast love endures forever!" (118:1) Or, "I lift up my eyes to the hills—from where will my help come? My help comes from the Lord, who made heaven and earth." (121:1-2)

Stories abound of despondent people, who checked into motels across America and in their desperation opened up the Gideon Bible in their desk drawer. With heavy hearts and tear filled eyes they read words of hope, where God revived their souls. Turning away from energy draining self-centeredness, God directed them to Jesus Christ, who gave them new life.

The rich guidance found in the book of Proverbs enlarges every soul willing to discover its magnificence. The whole world would be transformed into a Garden of Eden, if every mind were informed by and every heart lived out this glorious book. Through scripture God guides us in our behavior.

Americans today are looking for a word from God. Millions are looking to the stars to tell them what God has in store for them, so 1400 newspapers carry horoscopes to satisfy this need. The name of an astrologer is given on television, and for 95 cents a minute, she will give you a personal forecast of what the stars predict for you.

The true source of life from God is found in scripture. God has given us the Bible as his written word, and it is a great privilege to have this as our life textbook. This is our manual for living. A fundamental way God is touching the human heart is through the Bible.

❧ ❧ ❧

Dear God, thank you so much for the Bible. Help me to open my life to your Spirit through it. Enable me to discipline myself to read it daily, and to let you give me new hope through it. In Jesus' name. Amen

I want to be more faithful in letting God speak to me through the Bible.

Hope When We Are Wronged

"'Vengeance is mine, I will repay, says the Lord.'" Romans 12:19b

We all experience the pain of having been taken advantage of. Without being paranoid, everyone knows the feeling of being wronged. God gives us hope in times of feeling stepped on.

Jacob's father, Isaac, sent him to his homeland of Haran to find a wife. In those days, it was common to marry a relative, and Jacob's father, Isaac, specifically told him to find his mother's brother, Laban, in Haran and marry one of his daughters. He traveled many miles to Haran, when he came to a well, where shepherds were grazing their sheep. He asked where they came from, and they said, "We are from Haran." He asked, "Do you know Laban son of Nahor?" They said, "We do." and he inquired, "Is it well with him?" They said, "Yes, and here is his daughter Rachel coming with the sheep."

Jacob helped Rachel water her sheep, and then he kissed her and wept aloud. He told her he was her aunt Rebekah's son. Rachel ran and told her father, Laban, who invited Jacob to live with them. Jacob loved Rachel, and offered to work seven years, so he could have her as his wife. Laban agreed. After seven years passed, Jacob said, "Give me my wife that I may go into her, for my time is completed." Jacob agreed, and a big wedding party was planned. But that night, when Jacob was in his dark honeymoon bedroom or tent waiting for Rachel, Laban sent in his older daughter, Leah, who was also a beautiful woman. Apparently Leah spoke not a word throughout the darkened night, because the next morning Jacob was shocked to find he had spent it not with Rachel but with her older sister, Leah.

The next morning Jacob challenged Laban asking why he did this to him, and Laban said, "It is our custom that the oldest daughter must get married first." So, Jacob agreed to work another seven years for Rachel as well, and then Jacob was married to both Leah and Rachel.

Jacob avoided the temptation to retaliate in being wronged, but simply humbled himself to do the next step necessary to achieve his goal. He went right back to work. To take the creative, positive step of moving forward is the best way out of being wronged. Looking back with anger and allowing bitterness to fester in our hearts is a dead end street. Instead of wishing to even scores it is always good to remember, "Vengeance is mine, I will replay, says the Lord." Knowing God is on our side, and God will take care of wrong doing against us, is the best approach. There is hope even when we are wronged.

❧ ❧ ❧

Dear God, thank you so much for your grace in looking after my life. Thank you for freedom from bitterness against people, who have wronged me. In Jesus' name. Amen

I will hold no grudge against anybody.

Hope in Sour Family Relationships

"This time I will praise the Lord." Genesis 29:35b

Sometimes we find ourselves in difficult family situations where we see little hope. However, turning to God in those times fills us with the positive spirit and hope we desire.

It happened to Leah. Jacob did not love her, so "When the Lord saw that Leah was unloved, he opened her womb; but Rachel was barren." God had special pity on Leah by giving her children. She had three sons, and after each one, Leah said, "surely now my husband will love me." She thought giving her husband children would finally make him love her and bring her happiness. But, it didn't. Jacob loved her no more than before, but gave all of his attention to Rachel. And Leah continued to be unhappy. Finally, she had a fourth son, and now she said, "This time I will praise the Lord." She meant, "Even though my husband will not spend time with me, I will find fulfillment in God. I will praise the Lord and find my happiness in him."

Many Americans believe families bring supreme happiness. Certainly God made families for happiness. Having families is immensely satisfying. To have parents, brothers, sisters, children, aunts and uncles, people close to us for many years is so fulfilling. It brings deep joy. Holidays bring families together for glorious gatherings.

But what happens when we put all our trust in families, and expect to have all of our happiness come from them? Families develop problems. Often rejection comes from within them. They can hurt us deeply. If we expect all our happiness from marriage, the bridge of that institution is not able to hold us up alone. Marriages break up in divorce. Spouses die.

If your equation for happiness is, "my family and me alone", you are in big potential trouble. In fact, if you put God first and humble yourself before him, your family will be much happier, because you will do for it what God wants. As a godly man or woman you will be able to make much bigger sacrifices for your family, and you will be much more loving to them. You will pray for your family, and God will make you a more loving person because of it. If you humbly worship God, he will give you grace and make you more patient, kind and understanding. Families of genuinely godly fathers and mothers are the happiest families can be.

ﷺ ﷺ ﷺ

Dear God, thank you so much for my family, and give me grace, however, to allow you to be first in my life. Help me to humble myself before you, so your love can flow more freely into my family through me. In Jesus' name. Amen

I want to love my family most deeply by putting God first.

Hope in Receiving Wisdom from God

"If any of you is lacking in wisdom, ask God, who gives to all generously and ungrudgingly, and it will be given you." James 1:5

We all enjoy watching a highly intelligent person perform masterfully at an activity. In the eyes of the world intelligence is the supreme gift, but in the eyes of God it is wisdom. The world advertises the intelligence of children on bumper stickers, but God praises wisdom in the heart and mind. Each person has the hope of receiving this wisdom.

The book of Proverbs asserts, "wisdom is better than jewels, and all that you may desire cannot compare with her." There is nothing more important in life than to have understanding to make right choices.

That understanding comes from knowing who God is and who we are. The book of Proverbs says, "The fear of the Lord is the beginning of wisdom, and the knowledge of the Holy One is insight." (9:10) Living in awe of God provides us with the source of wisdom. That is how life fits together, knowing God grants insight as we humbly walk with him.

Wisdom has to do with making choices for behavior, as James wrote, "Show by your good life that your works are done with gentleness born of wisdom." (3:13b) He alludes to earthly wisdom that brings "envy and selfish ambition" where there will be "disorder and wickedness of every kind. But the wisdom from above is first pure, then peaceable, gentle, willing to yield, full of mercy and good fruits, without a trace of partiality or hypocrisy."

The wisdom that comes from God is very different than worldly wisdom in that it acknowledges everything comes from God. God has all wisdom and understanding. This highest wisdom includes faith and obedience to God.

How do we get the wisdom for our daily living? James wrote, "If any of you is lacking in wisdom, ask God, who gives to all generously and ungrudgingly, and it will be given you." (1:5) This invitation to come to God, asking for understanding and direction in life, is open to all. God will lovingly give wisdom to make right choices, and to walk in the most honorable paths. However, James also exhorts, " But ask in faith, never doubting, for the one who doubts is like a wave of the sea, driven and tossed by the wind..." (1:6) Ask sincerely, believing God is faithful to the promise to give is important.

৵৹ ৵৹ ৵৹

God of wisdom, please help me to be wise. Enable me to understand how to live my life in the most loving and honorable manner, which will glorify you and be the greatest blessing to myself. In Jesus' name. Amen

I will ask God for wisdom to live my life most fruitfully.

Hope in Bringing People to Christ

"Then Jesus said to Simon, 'Do not be afraid; from now on you will be catching people.'" Luke 5:10d

The world would be a jungle without Christianity. The American civilization would be immeasurably more self-centered and society more evil without disciples of Jesus Christ leavening moral standards with those of God. Therefore, it brings wonderful hope to be involved in discipling people for Jesus Christ.

On one occasion when Jesus was in Peter's boat, he told him to put it out into the deeper water and put down his nets for fish. Peter answered, "Master, we have worked all night long but have caught nothing. Yet if you say so, I will let down the nets." Peter thought it was futile to try now, when they had failed all night.

Though Simon was reluctant to obey Jesus to put his nets out, he did it, and Luke writes, "When they had done this, they caught so many fish that their nets were beginning to break. So they signaled their partners in the other boat to come and help them. And they came and filled both boats, so that they began to sink."

Peter was so amazed with their catch, "he fell down at Jesus' knees, saying, 'Go away from me, Lord, for I am a sinful man!'" Peter was blown away by what happened. Never had he seen anything like this, so it was obvious Jesus was a very special person.

Jesus said to Peter, "Do not be afraid; from now on you will be catching people.'" But why did Jesus say, "Do not be afraid?" Was it because Peter had been so humbled by all the fish they caught, and he fell on his knees before Jesus? Or, was it connected with the next words, "Do not be afraid; from now on you will be catching people." Peter was to be a witness to others, and in the New Testament, the Greek word for witness is the same as the word for martyr. Tradition says Peter and the other disciples were all martyred for their faith. Because they believed in Jesus Christ and spread that word, they were executed.

There are many people in our day needing the word of God. It is the same today as it was beside the Sea of Galilee on that very day. When we connect someone with Jesus Christ, they receive new life, and that makes them more than they could ever be on their own. We have new life of grace to offer. Jesus needs us to offer this gift to others.

Dear God, thank you for the persons who touched my life leading me to put my faith in Jesus Christ. Help me do the same for others, so more will come to know the new and wonderful life available in Jesus Christ. In his name. Amen

I will bear witness for Jesus Christ with my life today.

Hope Through Talking with God

"...Jesus took with him Peter and John and James, and went up on the mountain to pray." Luke 9:28b

It was toward the end of Jesus' life that he took his inner circle of disciples up the mountain to spend time in prayer. "And while he was praying, the appearance of his face changed, and his clothes became dazzling white." Luke 9:29 While Jesus prayed he met God with such wonder that his face was transfigured, and his clothes became sparkling white. He became a different person right before the disciples' very eyes.

Luke tells us more than any other Gospel writer about Jesus' prayer life. He tells us that after Jesus was baptized, he was praying. Then he heard a voice from heaven saying, "You are my Son, the Beloved; with you I am well pleased." (3:21) In chapter 11 Luke writes, "(Jesus) was praying in a certain place, and after he had finished, one of his disciple said to him, 'Lord, teach us to pray, as John taught his disciples.'" Then Jesus proceeded to teach them what we call the Lord's Prayer.

Jesus found the power and glory of God through prayer, and that is how you and I also find God most profoundly. Through talking with God, God's spirit touches our lives most deeply. Prayer is free talk that is not cheap. As Jesus was transformed, he became somebody different through prayer, so we are most changed through talking with God.

Prayer is communication with God. We talk with God the same way we talk with each other. We use the same words we use with people. Prayer ought to be a natural conversation. Prayer words with God are no different than people words. As we talk out loud so people can hear us, we often talk out loud with God. But when we talk aloud to God, it is not so he can hear us, but so we can better concentrate. Usually we can focus better if we can hear our words.

God knows everything within us, so we can also pray silently within our own hearts and minds. While it is dark Christians over the whole world, lie in bed offering their prayers to God in the quiet of their minds. During difficult meetings at work sitting around a table, you can kneel at the altar of your heart offering a prayer to God and no one will know what you are doing. But God will answer you, and that meeting will go better.

ﻼﻼﻼ

Dear God, thank you so much for the amazing gift of prayer. You are incredibly wonderful to allow us to talk with you as a friend. Lord Jesus, I open my life to you to receive your grace and kindness through prayer. In your name. Amen

I want to accept all the grace God has for me, as I commune with God.

Hope in Saying 'No' to Bodily Desire

"Then Jesus was led up by the Spirit into the wilderness to be tempted by the devil." Matthew 4:1

We all struggle with bodily desire, and there is great hope in learning to saying "no" to it.

After his baptism Jesus heard the voice of God say, "This is my Son, the Beloved, with whom I am well pleased." He must have felt very affirmed. As happens often in life, just after a great victory while living in the euphoria of triumph, evil attacks us. It is as though we are most vulnerable in times when our egos could become inflated with success. This reminds us to fight to keep our egos in control and to seek humility from God in times of great victory.

After Jesus was baptized Matthew writes, "Then Jesus was led up by the Spirit into the wilderness to be tempted by the devil. He fasted forty days and forty nights, and afterwards he was famished." (4:1-2)

At this point Satan came to tempt Jesus three times, and the temptations presented to Jesus are presented to each of us. The first temptation every human struggles is to say, "no" to bodily desires. Jesus was hungry, so the tempter said, "If you are the Son of God, command these stones to become loaves of bread. If you are really the one they say you are, make bread out of these stones." God had lead Jesus into the wilderness for a time of fasting, and if Jesus turned the stones to bread, which he could do, he would undercut God's will for him at this moment. And Satan used this basic bodily need to do it.

We are all tempted by evil to satisfy our bodily desires, so how do we handle these temptations? Jesus dealt with his by telling Satan, "It is written, 'one does not live by bread alone, but by every word that comes from the mouth of God.'" The mind cannot be occupied by two thoughts, so to overcome bodily temptations we can focus the mind on God. Thoughts about eating can be replaced with thoughts about God. When the mind becomes preoccupied with drinking liquor, fill it with God. As sexual thoughts preoccupy our minds, they can be driven out with thoughts about God. The hand that guards the door to the heart is in the mind.

ﷺ ﷺ ﷺ

Dear God, thank you for the gift of discipline to have control over my body. It is so wonderful to manage it, instead of having its appetites run my life. Help me be focused in taking care of this physical temple God gave me. In Jesus' name. Amen

I am going to say "no" today to acts that could hurt my body.

Hope in Overcoming Power Hunger

"Again, the devil took him to a very high mountain and showed him all the kingdoms of the world and their splendor; and he said to him, 'All these I will give you, if you will fall down and worship me.'" Matthew 4:8-9

All humans are tempted by power. God told Adam and Eve not to eat of the fruit in the middle of the Garden of Eden or they would die. Satan in the form of a snake tempted Eve in the garden saying to her, "You will not die, for God knows that when you eat of it your eyes will be opened, and you will be like God, knowing good and evil." The temptation to become like God and have the power of God was too great, and she ate. Her bait and enticement is that of each of us. We would like the power of God, so we don't have to lean on him.

The third temptation Satan presented Jesus in his wilderness experience is common to all, as it is the promise of power. After Jesus had rejected the first two temptations, Satan's final effort to get Jesus' allegiance was to take him to a very high mountain. It was one of those look out mountains, where you could see three states from one point. On a clear day Jesus was able to see many tens of miles in every direction. Satan said to him, "All these I will give you, if you will fall down and worship me. Jesus, here is what every full, red-blooded human being wants. You can be the ruler over all this land, and all the people on it, if you just bow down and honor me."

Power, which makes people drunk, comes in all forms. Power within a company can give authority over tens, hundreds or thousands of lives. Money power can make people feel totally independent, able to do all they wish. Then there is the power of personal relationships whether in family, church, neighborhood or friends.

If you are having temptations with power issues, read Paul's antidote daily for a month, and God will help you get over your hunger for power: "let the same mind be in you that was in Christ Jesus, who, though he was in the form of God, did not regard equality with God as something to be exploited, but emptied himself, taking the form of a slave, being born in human likeness. And being found in human form, he humbled himself and became obedient to the point of death—even death on a cross." (Philippians 2:5-8)

ℯℓℯ ℯℓℯ ℯℓℯ

Dear God, thank you for the gift of humility that washes away hunger for power, and I am grateful that in humility there is real power. It is the power over self, which brings us victory. In Jesus' name. Amen

Today I will bow before God and live in God's power.

Hope in Letting God be Number One

"Now therefore revere the Lord, and serve him in sincerity and in faithfulness; put away the gods that your ancestors served beyond the River and in Egypt, and serve the Lord." Joshua 24:14

There is hope in letting God be number one in our lives. Just as we have a biological age, we also have a spiritual age, and both are determined by choices. Choosing what kind of food we eat, and whether we will exercise or not, will affect our biological age. Although genes are important, our choice of lifestyle is also very significant. That means we are not strapped by genetics. We can make decisions that give us different bodies and lifestyles than our parents had.

Choices are also utterly important spiritually. Moses was not allowed to enter the Promised Land, but God used Joshua to lead his people into Canaan. When they got there, Joshua said to the people, "Now therefore revere the Lord, and serve him in sincerity and in faithfulness; put away the gods that your ancestors served..." (Josh 24:14) "Choose this day whom you will serve..." Joshua speaks those same words to us, as we step across the many thresholds of new experiences. Many gods present themselves to us, and we constantly have to choose whom we will serve. There are many gods, but only one living God. Jesus said, you cannot serve two masters. Anything that diverts attention from serving God is evil.

Our most important choice as we grow in years is to determine, who will get our allegiance. What will we follow in life. A lawyer asked Jesus one day, "Teacher, which commandment in the law is the greatest?" The Lord quoted from his Bible, "'You shall love the Lord your God with all your heart, and with all your soul, and with all your mind.'" (Matt. 22:37) This is the greatest commandment. Nothing in life is more important than following God, and making him the center of our intentions, our attitudes and our thoughts.

To maintain good, mature spiritual age requires that we allow the Holy Spirit to flow through our lives. God has to fill the capillaries of our very being. The Holy Spirit has to flow through our veins, so there is spiritual activity. Our arteries cannot be clogged with hatred, despair or negativism, because that is hurtful to our spiritual health. When our spiritual veins are not open to let love and grace flow through them, we become spiritual sluggards. There is no graceful activity. No love flows from us. Our families and friends begin noticing that we are no longer vibrant.

Dear God, I want you to control my entire life. When that happens; everything else falls beautifully in place. Thank you for wonderful grace to make my life so joyous and peaceful, when I let you have the reins of it. In Jesus' name. Amen

I will make God number one today and every day of my life.

Day 93

Hope Through Physical Healing

"But Peter said, 'I have no silver or gold, but what I have I give you;
in the name of Jesus Christ of Nazareth, stand up and walk.'" Acts 3:6

The body of every human malfunctions at various times in life requiring healing, and there is hope, because Dr. God is still in the healing business.

During the early days of the church, two of Jesus' disciples, Peter and John, were going to the Temple at three in the afternoon to pray. To get there they had to go through the gate called Beautiful. A certain man lame from birth was carried to that gate, where many passed daily, where he would beg for money. As Peter and John came along, he asked them for some cash. Something to help keep him alive. Peter and John stopped, and Peter gazed piercingly into the man's eyes, and said, "Look at us." The man returned the intense look hoping to get some money. But Peter said, "I have no silver or gold, but what I have I give you; in the name of Jesus Christ of Nazareth, stand up and walk."

Peter took him by the right hand and helped him get up. Instantly his feet and ankles were strengthened. At first he walked haltingly unbelieving what happened to him. But when his feet held him up, and he realized this was for real then he began leaping up and down. A smile covered his face, and he began praising God. He had not been inside the Temple for years, so he entered with Peter and John.

Usually people entering the Temple came quietly and subdued for prayer, so they were astounded to see a man excited. Jumping up and down and praising God. They saw it was the lame beggar to whom they had often given a few bucks because they felt sorry for him. Luke writes, "They were filled with wonder and amazement at what had happened to him." What had these people seen? They saw God giving the green light to a man, who had lived a whole life in front of a stop sign.

God is still in the healing business today, and God does it in various ways. God is best able to heal an unstressed body, so when the body has pain or discomfort, first pray, "Lord Jesus Christ, relax my body. Lord Jesus Christ, relax my body." With eyes closed pray that prayer for five minutes, and God will remove the stress to allow faster healing. But, also asking God to directly heal the body is putting our faith into practice. God the miracle maker is bringing physical wholeness today giving hope.

ᐧᐧ ᐧᐧ ᐧᐧ

Great Physician, I thank you for your healing power, and ask that you will always make me mindful of it. Enable me to bring my body to you for wholeness. And, help me to eat wisely and to exercise so your Holy Spirit can enhance my health. In Jesus' name. Amen

I will bring my body to God for constant physical wholeness.

Hope in Listening

"Now the Lord came and stood there, calling as before, 'Samuel! Samuel!'
And Samuel said, 'Speak, for your servant is listening.'" I Samuel 3:10

One of the great problems in every age is listening. We get so wrapped up in our own concerns that we tune out the world. Our own thoughts preoccupy us, so it is hard for something from the outside to penetrate them. We have hope, when we have ears able to hear and minds able to comprehend.

After Hannah prayed often for a child, God granted her wish. A son, Samuel, was born to her and Elkanah, and out of her deep gratitude to God for this gift, she promised this son to God. As soon as he was weaned, Hannah gave him to Eli, the high priest, to help in the temple. Scripture says, "Now the boy Samuel continued to grow both in stature and in favor with the Lord and with the people." (I Samuel 2:26) Almost identical words were used by Luke to describe Jesus, who would follow Samuel by about 1000 years.

According to Jewish tradition, Samuel was twelve, when living in the Temple serving Eli, the high priest. They slept in different quarters, and one night Samuel heard a voice, "Samuel! Samuel!" he immediately got up and ran to Eli saying, "Here I am." Eli said, "I did not call; lie down again." A second time, Samuel heard his name called, "Samuel!" Once more he ran to the elderly high priest, asking what he wanted. Eli responded once more, "I did not call, my son; lie down again." When it happened a third time, Eli realized God was calling Samuel, so he said to him, "Go lie down; and if he calls you, you shall say, 'Speak, Lord, for your servant is listening.'" Samuel went back to bed, and once more the Lord called his name, "Samuel! Samuel! And Samuel said, 'Speak for your servant is listening.'"

Developing and maintaining listening skills is fundamental to a good life. In order to be an effective person, one has to become a good listener. This is true within families. Good marriages and parenting skills are dependent upon being able to listen. Many a husband or wife has been frustrated, because it seemed as though the other didn't hear what was said. The path of listening has to go both ways for parents and children to get along with each other. Naturally, one can't be a good student without being a good listener. In the work place, it is the listening person, who gets promoted.

※ ※ ※

Dear God, thank you for listening to me, and help me to be a good listener as well. Allow me to stop my own thoughts, when engaged in conversations within my family or with friends, so I can hear what they are saying. Enable me to understand, that listening is important to loving. In Jesus' name. Amen

I am going to focus my mind to be a great listener.

Hope in God's Universal Call

"This is right and is acceptable in the sight of God our Savior, who desires everyone to be saved and to come to the knowledge of the truth." I Timothy 2:3-4

Wonderful hope fills the soul knowing we serve a glorious God, who wants to embrace all humanity. The heart is comforted to know that God loves every human being on the globe called earth, so God yearns for all to walk in fellowship with him.

God's inclusion of all was reflected in Jesus' calling Matthew, a tax collector, to be a disciple. That was a radical step. Up to now he had called fishermen, people of a decent profession. They provided food for society, and were considered good folk. But tax collectors were viewed as evil and scurrilous. For Matthew to become a disciple was risky for Jesus, because of Matthew's association and reputation.

Matthew invited Jesus to his home for dinner. Mark writes, "And as he sat at dinner in Levi's house, many tax collectors and sinners were also sitting with Jesus and his disciples.... for there were many who followed him." Religious leaders of the day were hanging around Jesus. Some were curious, and others who were cynically motivated tried to find reasons to criticize and condemn him.

Standing around the back of the room, these religious leaders, known as Pharisees, said to a couple of disciples, "Why does he eat with tax collectors and sinners?" Overhearing what they said, Jesus answered, "Those who are well have no need of a physician, but those who are sick; I have come to call not the righteous but sinners." Why did Jesus mix with people, who were considered outsiders? And what was he saying, when he said he came to call sinners?

Jesus is saying he came into the world to call all to follow God. Jesus came to bring all people into the kingdom of God, whereas the Pharisees wanted to exclude. Jesus said, "For God so loved the world that he gave his only Son, so that *everyone* who believes in him may not perish but may have eternal life." An old hymn says, "Whosoever will may come." Paul wrote in his first letter to Timothy, God "desires everyone to be saved and to come to the knowledge of truth." (I Tim. 2:4) God wants everyone in his heavenly party.

Jesus mixed with the outcasts not only because God wants to include them, but also because God is able to redeem them and make them whole. God can change people, and is in the people changing business.

പെ പെ പെ

Dear God, thank you that you love all and want salvation for everyone. My heart is touched to know that you want no one lost, but for all to know intimacy with you. Thank you for putting your eternal, loving and precious arms around everyone. In Jesus' name. Amen

What can I do to help everyone to know God?

Hope Through the Church

*"Christ loved the church and gave himself up for her,
in order to make her holy..." Ephesians 5:25b, 26a*

When God established the church of Jesus Christ, God created an organism that would change the world. Despite its many failures and weaknesses, the church is the cornerstone of every society where it is found. By the grace of God the church infuses life to communities as the heart pumps life giving oxygen throughout the body.

The church fills a critical need in society. The church of Jesus Christ provides not only guidance but also moral strength to people, so the church is very important in every country. The social contributions of Christians through the church in America are enormous. God has established a high percentage of the nation's colleges and universities through the church. Christians have also built a significant number of the nation's hospitals and nursing homes. In addition, the church created a large percentage of the country's agencies for children, and virtually every homeless shelter in America exists by funding and staffing from Christians.

The church of Jesus Christ gives hope to people around the world. Wherever it establishes communities of faith, it also creates health care facilities, schools, agricultural training centers and other efforts to lift the level of life for people. The church has always been in the forefront abroad providing tents and medical care in refugee camps. When hunger crises hit a nation, the church is there first distributing food.

However, all of this happens only when the church's members realize all players are important. Paul wrote that the church is like the human body. Every part is significant. He said, "Indeed, the body does not consist of one member but of many. If the foot would say, 'Because I am not a hand, I do not belong to the body,' that would not make it any less a part of the body." (I Cor. 12:15) In verse 17, he writes, "If the whole body were an eye, where would the hearing be?"

Paul writes that the church is like the human body. Every role in the church is very important. No matter what your role in the church, you are highly significant. He asks in verse 19, "If all were a single member, where would the body be? As it is, there are many members, yet one body." Like the body the church has many members fulfilling various functions, and everyone is important. Whether it is cleaning the kitchen, ushering, teaching, doing youth work, singing or playing an instrument. Every ministry is to be regarded as significant. There are no second class citizens in the church just as there are no secondary parts of our bodies.

علي علي علي

Dear God, thank you for the work of the church around the whole world. I am grateful for its word of salvation, but also for its work of redemption. Use my energies through my church to make a difference for Christ. In his name. Amen

I will pour out my energies, so God can change the world through me.

Hope by Taking Care of Ourselves

"Or do you not know that your body is a temple of the Holy Spirit within you, which you have from God, and that you are not your own? For you were bought with a price; therefore glorify God in your body." I Corinthians 6:19

God has given you to yourself as a gift, and now taking care of yourself is your responsibility. Hope for the best life you can have depends a great deal on how well you care for yourself.

As our very beings are a gift from God, so are our bodies. God not only gave us bodies, but God resides in them. The apostle Paul wrote, "… do you not know that your body is a temple of the Holy Spirit within you, which you have from God, and that you are not your own? For you were bought with a price; therefore glorify God in your body." (I Cor. 6:19) If our bodies are the temple of God, what does that say to us? If they really belong to God, and are only on loan to us, how should we treat them?

First exercise is important. There is abundant information available, that on average, people who exercise live longer. If a non-Christian and a Christian both live the same kind of life styles, the exercising non-Christian will be healthier and live longer than the non exercising Christian. It makes no difference how young or old we are, exercising enables God to make us healthier and stronger and live longer. Not only is exercise good for us, but it also helps us control our weight. Dieting is helpful, but dieting and exercise together are most useful to maintain our weight.

Paul wrote to young Timothy about training himself in godliness, and wrote, "physical training is of some value." (I Tim. 4:8) Even though he went on to say that training ourselves in godliness is of most value, physical exercise is also important.

Not only is physical exercise important, but also if we take care of ourselves we will keep our stress level down, because stress can kill. We are told 80% of all illnesses are stress related. We Christians have to fight the American habit of trying to get more done than is humanly possible. Trying to accomplish too much is stressful. Reducing stress also involves maintaining loving relationships. When angry voices get raised in homes and work places, blood pressures go up, and nerves and muscles become tense.

How do you and I handle life's problems without their tearing us apart? Building down time into our schedules is important, when the mind, spirit and body can relax. Spending time in prayer is a tremendous gift that is totally free, and obviously is available to us every day.

Dear God, thank you for helping me take care of myself. Give me wisdom and discipline to do those things that will help me be the strongest and most wholesome person possible. In Jesus' name. Amen

I want to take care of my body, mind and spirit for the sake of Jesus Christ.

Hope in Practicing Our Faith

"(Jesus) said to her, 'Daughter, your faith has made you well; go in peace, and be healed of your disease.'" Mark 5:34

Telling of a woman, who had been suffering hemorrhages for twelve years, Mark writes, "She had endured much under many physicians, and had spent all that she had; and she was no better, but rather grew worse." After dealing with this terrible, embarrassing problem over a decade then "She…heard about Jesus…" She learned that he had given sight to the blind, freed paralytic legs, and restored people to sanity with healthy emotions by casting out demons. After running from doctor to doctor for 12 years, she realized that medicine, dealing with the body chemistry, had not worked.

"She heard about Jesus, and came up behind him in the crowd and touched his cloak, for she said, 'If I but touch his clothes, I will be made well.'" (Mark 5:27) This basic, hopeful practicing of our faith is available to every Christian: "If I but touch his clothes, I will be made well." If you touch God, he will heal you. When she put her faith into action, "Immediately her hemorrhage stopped; and she felt in her body that she was healed of her disease." There was a noticeable change in her chemistry, and God's doing that didn't just take place back then. What Jesus did 2000 years ago, he is doing still today.

Because we are made up of body, mind and spirit, when we get sick there are different ways of approaching our sickness. We can say, "My body is hurting. I am going to take some aspirin." Or, we can say, "My body is hurting, and I wonder what is causing it? Is it something in my spirit?" Most Americans do not ask the spirit question, when they get sick, because most Americans do not understand the inter-relationship between body and spirit in wholeness. When we do understand that our problem may be a spirit issue, then it becomes something we have to deal with. But it can be a body issue, when it is wise to see a doctor to take care of us.

When you are sick, practice your Christianity. Put it to work. Lean on God. What kind of healing do you need? Do you have a physical problem? Don't be ashamed of coming to Jesus asking for healing. Are you shut out of relationships? Do you need God to unite you to family? Or to a friend? Do you need healing of your soul?

❧ ❧ ❧

Great Healer, thank you for wanting me whole. I praise your name for the wholeness you want for all your children. Help me to act on my faith today to allow the fullness of grace to come into my life. In Jesus' name. Amen

Where do I need to practice my faith for healing today?

Hope in Unexpected Joys

"The kingdom of heaven is like treasure hidden in a field, which someone found and hid; then in his joy he goes and sells all that he has and buys that field." Matthew 13:44

The kingdom of God appears in the most surprising places and times. Our Lord said, "The kingdom of heaven is like treasure hidden in the field, which someone found and hid; then in his joy he goes and sells all that he has and buys that field."

In Jesus' day, there were banks, but ordinary people used the ground as their safety deposit box. They buried their money in fields. Wars were common in Palestine, and fighting often made people flee their homes. Sometimes they didn't' come back. Someone else came along years later, and found a pot of money while digging in that field. Wealth not his own came to him in a most unexpected place, and Jesus said the kingdom of God is like that. Often, when we least expect it, we see God ruling over people's lives in a wonderful way. God surprises us often making things happen for us that we did not expect. These God-incidences often spare us embarrassment as God bales us out of difficult situations. Many times God uses the right people to do something we did not expect, and grace catches us unaware again.

I saw the kingdom of God in a hotel on vacation. A mother at a continental breakfast was lovingly feeding her quadriplegic teenage son in a wheelchair, as I took my empty cup and plate to the wastebasket I stopped beside her and said, "Thank you for being a loving mother." God's love was so obviously ruling life through her.

During a senior luncheon conversation about sleep, one of the men said he always sleeps with one eye open. He went on to explain that he and his wife had a son born with a neurological problem that never allowed him to walk. He lived 25 years in a bed without taking a step, and his parents took turns caring for him. The mother by day, then she went to work after the father returned from his daytime job. At night as he watched over their son, the father said he slept with one eye open. The kingdom of God was in that home as these loving parents cared for an invalid son for 25 years. Surprisingly filled with profound grace they showered it upon a son, who could not respond to their kindnesses.

❧ ❧ ❧

Gracious God, I am so grateful that you rule so lovingly in my life. Thank you for breaking into my life with joyous surprises. Help me today to have eyes to see your grace manifesting itself. In Jesus' name. Amen

I will watch for God's surprises, and be humbly grateful as I see them.

Hope in Eternal Life with Jesus Christ

*"For the wages of sin is death, but the free gift of God is eternal life
in Christ Jesus our Lord." Romans 6:23*

The ultimate of hope of Christians is eternal life with God through faith in Jesus Christ. When death closes our eyelids for the last time, that is not the end of life for us, but rather the beginning of something far more glorious than the human mind can imagine.

One of the criminals crucified on a cross beside Jesus said to him, "Jesus, remember me when you come into your kingdom." (Luke 23:42) Jesus answered, "Truly I tell you today you will be with me in Paradise." In saying this, Jesus was saying more than simply, "You will be with me." Rather, you and I will recognize each other. There will be wonderful personal recognition in the next life. Furthermore, the movement into that unimaginable state of joy and goodness begins immediately upon death. There is no waiting in some intermediate state, but rather as Jesus said, "today, you will be with me in Paradise."

This gives us enormous hope for this life. Whatever struggles we are having are not the end, but victory is in sight for those who have eternal life in Jesus Christ. The gift of eternal life begins not at death, but rather at the point of trusting Jesus Christ. Eternal life eclipses time, and time is only a hair's breath on the scale of eternal life.

If we put our trust in Jesus Christ, there is nothing to fear. Trusting in Jesus Christ we are safe whether in this life or the next. The early Christians were willingly thrown to the lions knowing they could not inflict final hurt on them. Living with complete, glorious faith in eternal life frees us from fear of death to live life with confidence, energy and verve. Nothing can cause eternal hurt in this life. We may suffer setbacks that cause temporary pain, but they cannot inflict God separating hurt.

As the apostle Paul wrote to the Christians in Rome, "For I am convinced that neither death, nor life, nor angels, nor rulers, nor things present, nor things to come, nor power, nor height, nor depth, nor anything else in all creation, will be able to separate us from the love of God in Christ Jesus our Lord." (Romans 8:38-39)

Dear God, I am so deeply thankful for the gift of eternal life in Jesus Christ. My spirit is immersed with joy to know that your love wrapped around me in this life will lift me even to a more wonderful life in heaven. Help me to accept this gift to the core of my being, so I can walk with utter faith and excitement. In Jesus' name. Amen

I am free to live with confidence, because God has made all well through Jesus Christ both in this life and the next.